Cognitive Behavioural Therapy

FOR

DUMMIES®

PORTABLE EDITION

Cognitive Behavioural Therapy

FOR

DUMMIES®

PORTABLE EDITION

by Rhena Branch and Rob Willson

A John Wiley and Sons, Ltd, Publication

Cognitive Behavioural Therapy For Dummies® Portable Edition

Published by
John Wiley & Sons, Ltd
The Atrium
Southern Gate
Chichester
West Sussex
PO19 8SQ
England

E-mail (for orders and customer service enquires): cs-books@wiley.co.uk

Visit our Home Page on www.wiley.com

Copyright © 2011 John Wiley & Sons, Ltd, Chichester, West Sussex, England

Published by John Wiley & Sons, Ltd, Chichester, West Sussex

For general information on our other products and services, please contact our Customer Care Department within the U.S. at 877-762-2974, outside the U.S. at 317-572-3993, or fax 317-572-4002.

For technical support, please visit www.wiley.com/techsupport.

Wiley also publishes its books in a variety of electronic formats. Some content that appears in print may not be available in electronic books.

British Library Cataloguing in Publication Data: A catalogue record for this book is available from the British Library

ISBN: 978-1-119-97437-6 (paperback), 978-1-119-97493-2 (ebk), 978-1-119-97494-9 (ebk) 978-1-119-97495-6 (ebk)

Printed and bound in Great Britain by TJ International, Padstow, Cornwall

10 9 8 7 6 5 4 3 2 1

WILEY

About the Authors

Rhena Branch, MSc, Dip CBT, is an accredited CBT therapist and holds a post-graduate clinical supervision qualification. Rhena runs a private practice with offices in North and Central London. She also teaches and supervises on the MSc course in CBT/REBT at Goldsmith's College, University of London. Rhena treats general psychiatric disorders and has a special interest in eating disorders. *CBT For Dummies* (second edition) is Rhena's fifth publication and she currently has two further books in press.

Rob Willson, BSc, MSc, Dip SBHS, currently divides the majority of his work time between private practice and conducting research on Body Dysmorphic Disorder at the Institute of Psychiatry, London. Previously he spent twelve years working at the Priory Hospital, North London where he was a therapist and therapy services manager. He also trained numerous CBT therapists over a seven-year period at Goldsmith's College, University of London. Rob's main clinical interests are anxiety and obsessional problems, and disseminating CBT principles through self-help. He has made several TV appearances including in the BBC documentary 'Too Ugly for Love'.

Dedication

For Felix and Atticus (from Rhena)

For Emma and Lucy (from Rob)

Authors' Acknowledgements

From Rhena: It's great to have the opportunity to produce a second edition of this book. My thanks to everyone involved at Wiley for your support and expert guidance throughout.

Thanks to Rob for your input into this and other projects.

Immense gratitude as always to my boys, for everything.

From Rob: I am grateful to Wiley for approaching (and eventually persuading) me to take on the first edition of *CBT For Dummies;* I know it has made CBT more accessible for many people. I would like to thank huge number of clients, clinicians, trainees, people interested in CBT, and people courageous enough to embark upon a course of self-help, not only for purchasing the first edition but also for giving so much positive feedback about the book.

Thanks to Rhena for her revisions and driving this second edition forward.

From both of us: Many researchers, fellow therapists and authors have influenced our understanding and practice of CBT over the years and therefore the content in this book. Founding fathers, Albert Ellis and Aaron T. Beck, of course merit special mention. Others include (in no specific order): Ray DiGiuseppe, Mary-Anne Layden, Jacqueline Persons, David A. Clarke, Adrian Wells, Stanley Rachman, Paul Salkovskis, Christine Padesky, Michael Neenan, David Veale, David M. Clark, David Burns, Kevin Gournay and many more. Special thanks goes to Windy Dryden for his extensive writings and for teaching us both so much.

Finally, a genuine thank you to all our clients (past and present) for allowing us to get to know you and learn from you.

Publisher's Acknowledgements

We're proud of this book; please send us your comments through our Dummies online registration form located at www.dummies.com/register/.

Some of the people who helped bring this book to market include the following:

Commissioning, Editorial, and Media Development

Project Editor: Simon Bell

Commissioning Editor: Nicole Hermitage

Assistant Editor: Ben Kemble

Developer/Copy Editor: Kate O'Leary

Technical Editor: David Kingdon

Publisher: David Palmer

Production Manager: Daniel Mersey

Cover Photos: ©Rphotos / Alamy

Cartoons: Rich Tennant
(www.the5thwave.com)

Composition Services

Project Coordinator: Kristie Rees

Layout and Graphics: Christin Swinford

Proofreader: Dwight Ramsey

Indexer: Potomac Indexing, LLC

Brand Reviewer: Zoë Wykes

Publishing and Editorial for Consumer Dummies

Diane Graves Steele, Vice President and Publisher, Consumer Dummies

Joyce Pepple, Acquisitions Director, Consumer Dummies

Kristin A. Cocks, Product Development Director, Consumer Dummies

Michael Spring, Vice President and Publisher, Travel

Kelly Regan, Editorial Director, Travel

Publishing for Technology Dummies

Andy Cummings, Vice President and Publisher, Dummies Technology/General User

Composition Services

Debbie Stailey, Director of Composition Services

Contents at a Glance

Contents

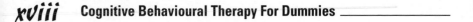

Introduction

● ●

*C*ognitive behavioural therapy, or CBT, is growing in popularity as an efficient and long lasting treatment for many different types of psychological problem. If the word 'psychological' sends you running from the room screaming, try to consider the term referring to problems that affect your emotional rather than your physical sense of wellbeing. At some point in your life, something's going to go a bit wrong with your body. So why on earth do humans assume that their minds and emotions should be above the odd hiccup, upset, or even more serious difficulty?

This book gives you a comprehensive introduction to the theory and application of CBT techniques. Although we don't have the space to go into nitty-gritty specifics about how to use CBT to overcome every type of emotional or psychological problem, we do try to lead you in a helpful direction. We believe all the CBT principles and strategies outlined in this book can improve your life and help you to stay healthy, regardless of whether you've worked with or are currently working with a psychiatrist or other psychological professional.

In addition, whether you think your problems are minimal, you're living the life of Riley, you feel mildly depressed, or you've had years of uncomfortable psychological symptoms, CBT can help you. We ask you to be open-minded and to use the stuff in this book to make your life better and fuller.

About This Book

If you're embarking on a journey of self-help or self-improvement, we hope that this book provides a useful introduction to CBT techniques and will be of benefit to you. Depending on the degree of disruption and distress that your personal difficulties are causing you, this book may or may not be enough treatment to help you recover. The book may spur you on to get further help (Chapter 14 has more on seeking professional help) to really knock your emotional demons on the head. This book covers the following:

- ✔ The basics of using CBT as a scientifically tested and verified psychotherapeutic method of overcoming common emotional problems.

- ✔ Ways in which you can identify your problems and set specific goals for how you would rather be living your life.

- ✔ Techniques to identify errors in the way you may be thinking and to adopt more helpful thoughts, attitudes, philosophies, and beliefs.

- ✔ Behavioural experiments and strategies you can incorporate into your life to improve your day-to-day functioning.

- ✔ Information that can help you to understand, normalise, and address some common human problems. You may think that you're the only person in the world who feels and thinks the way you do. This book shows you that many of the problems you may be experiencing such as depression, anxiety, anger, and obsessions are in fact very common. You are not alone.

We hope that the whole experience will be at least a little entertaining in the process. So read on, welcome new concepts, and consider trying some of the ideas we offer in the book.

Conventions Used in This Book

To make your reading experience easier and to alert you to key words or points, we use certain conventions.

- ✔ *Italics* introduce new terms, underscore key differences in meaning between words, and highlight the most important aspects of a sentence or example.

- ✔ We use the terms 'him' in even-numbered chapters and 'her' in odd-numbered chapters when writing, with a view to incorporate gender equality.

 ✔ The case studies in the book are illustrative of actual clients we have treated and are not direct representations of any particular clients.

 ✔ **Bold** text is used to show the action part of numbered lists.

What You're Not to Read

This book is written in a rough order to help you progress from the basics of CBT on to more complex techniques and ideas. However, you can read the chapters in any order you like or just hit on the ones that cover subjects you think you want to know more about.

To make your reading experience even easier, we identify 'skippable' material:

 ✔ **Sidebars:** Within most chapters, we include sidebars of shaded text. These sidebars contain interesting titbits of information or occasionally expand on a topic within the chapter. Read them if they sound interesting to you and skip them if they don't.

 ✔ **Our acknowledgements:** Probably pretty boring to the average reader.

Foolish Assumptions

In writing this little tome, we make the following assumptions about you, dear reader:

 ✔ You're human.

 ✔ As a human, you're likely at some stage in your life to experience some sort of emotional problem that you'd like to surmount.

 ✔ You've heard about CBT, or are intrigued by CBT, or have had CBT suggested to you by a doctor, friend, or mental health professional as a possible treatment for your specific difficulties.

✔ Even if you don't think you're particularly in need of CBT right now, you want to discover more about some of the principles outlined in this book.

✔ You think that your life is absolutely fine right now, but you want to find interesting and useful information in the book that will enhance your life further.

✔ You're keen to find out whether CBT may be helpful to someone close to you.

✔ You're studying CBT and want to use this book as a 'hands on' adjunct to your training.

How This Book Is Organised

This book is divided into five parts and 17 chapters. The table of contents lists subheadings with more information about every chapter, but the following describes the major sections of the book.

Part 1: Introducing CBT Basics

This part gives you a pretty good idea about what CBT consists of and how the techniques differs from other forms of psychotherapy. 'You think how you feel' is a good way of summing up CBT, and the chapters in this part expand on this simple idea. We explain common thinking errors as well as ways to counteract skewed thinking. You discover the basic CBT model of emotional disturbance and find out more about how you can make positive changes, even when your circumstances and other people in your life are unlikely to change for the better.

Part II: Charting the Course: Defining Problems and Setting Goals

This part helps you to define your emotional problems more accurately, see where your problems are springing from, and develop solid goals for your emotional future. Some of your valiant attempts to deal with your worries, terrors, and ideas about yourself are frequently counterproductive in the long term. These chapters explore this notion and give you ideas about more productive alternative strategies to produce long-term benefits.

Part III: Putting CBT into Action

Actions speak louder than words, and believe us when we say that actions also produce better results than words alone. Correcting your thinking is an important endeavour, but all your efforts to think healthily can fall apart at the seams unless you translate new beliefs into new action. The chapters in this part set out some good ways to test your new ways of thinking, strengthen healthy new beliefs, and promote helpful emotional responses to life, the universe, and everything else. If you don't believe us, try out the ideas for yourself! We also explore some common human difficulties such as anxiety and obsessional problems, addictions and poor body image.

Part IV: Looking Backwards and Moving Forwards

'But CBT ignores my past!' is an oft-heard complaint by individuals new to CBT. So we're here to tell you that CBT does not ignore your past. Yes, CBT concentrates on how your *current* thinking and behaviour cause your *current* difficulties. This part aids you in recognising experiences from your past that may have led you to form certain types of beliefs about yourself, other people, and the world around you. Assigning updated, helpful, and more accurate meanings to past events really can make a difference to the way you experience life today. So read on!

Part V: The Part of Tens

This section of the book is part fun and part solid CBT stuff. Looking here first can help you connect to other parts of the book and provide quick and easy tips for healthier living, boosting your self-esteem the right way, and lightening up your attitudes towards yourself and life in general.

Icons Used in This Book

We use the following icons in this book to alert you to certain types of information that you can choose to read, commit to memory (and possibly interject into dinner party conversation), or maybe just utterly ignore:

This icon highlights practical advice for putting CBT into practice.

This icon is a cheerful, if sometimes urgent, reminder of important points to take notice of.

This icon marks out specific things to avoid or possible traps to keep your eye open for in your quest for better emotional health.

This icon highlights CBT terminology that may sound a bit like psychobabble but is commonly used by CBT practitioners.

This icon alerts you to stuff that has a bit of a philosophical basis and may need some mulling over in your spare time.

This icon indicates a CBT technique that you can try out in real life to see what results you get.

Where to Go from Here

We'd really like you to read everything in this book and then recommend it to all your friends and random people you meet on the street. Failing that, just use this book as your reference guide to CBT, dipping in and out of it as and when you need to.

Have a browse through the table of contents and turn to the chapters that look as if they may offer something helpful to you and your current difficulties.

Part I

Introducing CBT Basics

The 5th Wave   By Rich Tennant

"Let's see if we can identify some of the stress triggers in your life. You mentioned something about a large wolf that periodically shows up and attempts to blow your house down..."

In this part . . .

You'll get to grips with what CBT stands for and why it's such a hot topic among mental health professionals. You'll get a good idea of how your thinking about events leads to how you feel. We'll get you started on recognising and tackling your negative thought patterns, and give you some tips about exerting control over your attention.

Chapter 1

You Feel the Way You Think

In This Chapter

▶ Defining CBT

▶ Exploring the power of meanings

▶ Understanding how your thoughts lead to emotions and behaviours

▶ Getting acquainted with the ABC formula

*C*ognitive behavioural therapy – more commonly referred to as *CBT* – focuses on the way people think and act to help them with their emotional and behavioural problems.

Many of the effective CBT practices we discuss in this book should seem like everyday good sense. In our opinion, CBT does have some very straightforward and clear principles and is a largely sensible and practical approach to helping people overcome problems. However, human beings don't always act according to sensible principles, and most people find that simple solutions can be very difficult to put into practice sometimes. CBT can maximise on your common sense and help you to do the healthy things that you may sometimes do naturally and unthinkingly in a deliberate and self-enhancing way on a regular basis.

In this chapter we take you through the basic principles of CBT and show you how to use these principles to better understand yourself and your problems.

Using Scientifically Tested Methods

The effectiveness of CBT for various psychological problems has been researched more extensively than any other psychotherapeutic approach. CBT's reputation as a highly effective treatment is growing. Several studies reveal that CBT is more effective than medication alone for the treatment of anxiety and depression and many other disorders. People who have CBT relapse less often than those who have other forms of psychotherapy or take medication only.

CBT is growing in popularity. More and more physicians and psychiatrists refer their patients for CBT to help them overcome a wide range of problems with good results.

Understanding CBT

Cognitive behavioural therapy is a school of *psychotherapy* that aims to help people overcome their emotional problems.

- ✔ **Cognitive** means mental processes like thinking. The word 'cognitive' refers to everything that goes on in your mind including dreams, memories, images, thoughts and attention.

- ✔ **Behaviour** refers to everything that you do. This includes what you say, how you try to solve problems, how you act and avoidance. Behaviour refers to both action and inaction, for example biting your tongue instead of speaking your mind is still a behaviour even though you are trying *not* to do something.

- ✔ **Therapy** is a word used to describe a systematic approach to combating a problem, illness or irregular condition.

A central concept in CBT is that *you feel the way you think.* Therefore, CBT works on the principle that you can live more happily and productively if you're thinking in healthy ways. This principle is a very simple way of summing up CBT, and we have many more details to share with you later in the book.

Combining science, philosophy and behaviour

CBT is a powerful treatment because it combines scientific, philosophical and behavioural aspects into one comprehensive approach to understanding and overcoming common psychological problems.

✔ **Getting scientific.** CBT is scientific not only in the sense that it has been tested and developed through numerous scientific studies, but also in the sense that it encourages clients to become more like scientists. For example, during CBT, you may develop the ability to treat your thoughts as theories and hunches about reality to be tested (what scientists call *hypotheses*), rather than as facts.

✔ **Getting philosophical.** CBT recognises that people hold values and beliefs about themselves, the world and other people. One of the aims of CBT is to help people develop flexible, non-extreme and self-helping beliefs that help them adapt to reality and pursue their goals.

Your problems are not all just in your mind. Although CBT places great emphasis on thoughts and behaviour as powerful areas to target for change and development, it also places your thoughts and behaviours within a *context*. CBT recognises that you're influenced by what's going on around you and that your *environment* makes a contribution towards the way you think, feel and act. However, CBT maintains that you can make a difference to the way you feel by changing unhelpful ways of thinking and behaving – even if you can't change your environment. Incidentally, your environment in the context of CBT includes other people and the way they behave towards you. Your living situation, workplace dynamics or financial concerns are also features of your larger environment.

✔ **Getting active.** As the name suggests, CBT also strongly emphasises behaviour. Many CBT techniques involve changing the way you think and feel by modifying the way you behave. Examples include gradually becoming more active if you're depressed and lethargic, or facing your fears step by step if you're anxious. CBT also places emphasis on *mental behaviours*, such as worrying and where you focus your attention.

Progressing from problems to goals

A defining characteristic of CBT is that it gives you the tools to develop a *focused* approach. CBT aims to help you move from defined emotional and behavioural problems towards your goals of how you'd like to feel and behave. Thus, CBT is a goal-directed, systematic, problem-solving approach to emotional problems.

Making the Thought– Feeling Link

Like many people, you may assume that if something happens to you, the event *makes* you feel a certain way. For example, if your partner treats you inconsiderately, you may conclude that she *makes* you angry. You may further deduce that their inconsiderate behaviour *makes* you behave in a particular manner, such as sulking or refusing to speak to her for hours (possibly even days; people can sulk for a very long time!). We illustrate this common (but incorrect) causal relationship with the following formula. In this equation, the 'A' stands for a real or *actual* event – such as being rejected or losing your job. It also stands for an *activating* event that may or may not have happened. It could be a prediction about the future, such as 'I'm going to get the sack', or a memory of a past rejection, such as 'Hilary will dump me just like Judith did ten years ago!'. 'C' stands for *consequence*, which means the way you feel and behave in response to an actual or activating event.

A (*actual* or *activating* event) = C (emotional and behavioural *consequence*)

CBT encourages you to understand that your thinking or *beliefs* lie between the event and your ultimate feelings and actions. Your thoughts, beliefs and the meanings that you give to an event, produce your emotional and behavioural responses.

So in CBT terms, your partner does not *make* you angry and sulky. Rather, your partner behaves inconsiderately, and you assign a meaning to her behaviour such as 'she's doing this deliberately to upset me and she absolutely should not do this!' thus *making yourself* angry and sulky. In the next formula, 'B' stands for your *beliefs* about the event and the *meanings* you give to it.

A (*actual* or *activating* event) + B (*beliefs* and *meanings* about the event) = C (emotional and behavioural *consequence*)

This is the formula or equation that CBT uses to make sense of your emotional problems.

Emphasising the meanings you attach to events

The *meaning* you attach to any sort of event influences the emotional responses you have to that event. Positive events normally lead to positive feelings of happiness or excitement, whereas negative events typically lead to negative feelings like sadness or anxiety.

However, the meanings you attach to certain types of negative events may not be wholly accurate, realistic, or helpful. Sometimes, your thinking may lead you to assign extreme meanings to events, leaving you feeling disturbed

Tilda meets up with a nice man that she's contacted via an online dating agency. She quite likes him on their first date and hopes he'll contact her for a second meeting. Unfortunately, he doesn't. After two weeks of waiting eagerly by the computer, Tilda gives up and becomes depressed. The fact that the chap failed to ask Tilda out again *contributes* to her feeling bad. But what really *leads* to her acute depressed feelings is the meaning she's derived from his apparent rejection, namely: 'This proves I'm old, unattractive, past it and unwanted. I'll be a sad singleton for the rest of my life.'

As Tilda's example shows, drawing extreme conclusions about yourself (and others and the world at large) based on singular experiences can turn a bad *distressing* situation into a deeply *disturbing* one.

Psychologists use the word 'disturbed' to describe emotional responses that are unhelpful and cause significant discomfort to you. In CBT terminology, 'disturbed' means that an emotional or behavioural response is hindering rather than helping you to adapt and cope with a negative event.

For example, if a potential girlfriend rejects you after the first date (event), you may think 'This proves I'm unlikeable and undesirable' (meaning) and feel depressed (emotion).

CBT involves identifying thoughts, beliefs and meanings that are activated when you're feeling emotionally disturbed. If you assign less extreme, more helpful, more *accurate* meanings to negative events, you are likely to experience less extreme, less disturbing emotional and behavioural responses.

Thus, on being rejected after the first date (event), you could think 'I guess that person didn't like me that much; oh well – they're not the one for me' (meaning), and feel disappointment (emotion).

You can help yourself to figure out whether or not the meanings you're giving to a specific negative event are causing you disturbance by answering the following questions:

- ✔ **Is the meaning I'm giving to this event unduly extreme?** Am I taking a fairly simple event and deriving very harsh conclusions about myself (others and/or the future) from it?

- ✔ **Am I drawing global conclusions from this singular event?** Am I deciding that this one event defines me totally? Or that this specific situation indicates the course of my entire future?

- ✔ **Is the meaning I'm assigning to this event loaded against me?** Does this meaning lead me to feel better or worse about myself? Is it spurring me on to further goal-directed action or leading me to give in and curl up?

If your answer to these questions is largely 'yes', then you probably are disturbing yourself needlessly about a negative event. The situation may well be negative – but your thinking is making it even worse. In Chapters 2 and 3 we guide you toward correcting disturbance-creating thinking and help you to feel appropriate distress instead.

Consider the reactions of ten people

Different people can attach different meanings to a specific situation, resulting in the potential for a vast array of emotional reactions to one situation. For example, consider ten basically similar people who experience the same event, which is having their partner treat them inconsiderately. Potentially, they can have ten (or maybe more) different emotional responses to precisely the same event, depending on how they *think* about the event:

Person 1 attaches the meaning, 'That idiot has no right to treat me badly – who the hell do they think they are?' and feels angry.

Person 2 thinks, 'This lack of consideration means that my partner doesn't love me' and feels depressed.

Person 3 believes that 'This inconsideration must mean that my partner is about to leave me for someone else' and feels jealous.

Person 4 thinks, 'I don't deserve to be treated poorly because I always do my best to be considerate to my partner' and feels hurt.

Person 5 reckons the event means that 'I must have done something serious to upset my partner for them to treat me like this' and feels guilty.

Person 6 believes that 'This inconsideration is a sign that my partner is losing interest in me' and feels anxious.

Person 7 thinks, 'Aha! Now I have a good enough reason to break up with my partner, which I've been wanting to do for ages!' and feels happy.

Person 8 decides the event means that 'My partner has done a bad thing by treating me in this way, and I'm not prepared to put up with it' and feels annoyed.

Person 9 thinks, 'I really wish my partner had been more considerate because we're usually highly considerate of each other' and feels disappointed.

Person 10 believes that 'My partner must have found out something despicable about me to treat me in this way' and feels ashamed.

You can see from this example that very different meanings can be assigned to the same event and in turn produce very different emotional responses. Some emotional responses are healthier than others; we discuss this matter in depth in Chapter 5.

Acting out

The ways you think and feel also largely determine the way you *act*. If you feel depressed, you're likely to withdraw and isolate yourself. If you're anxious, you may avoid situations that you find threatening or dangerous. Your behaviours can be problematic for you in many ways, such as the following:

✔ **Self-destructive behaviours,** such as excessive drinking or using drugs to quell anxiety, can cause direct physical harm.

✔ **Isolating and mood-depressing behaviours,** such as staying in bed all day or not seeing your friends, increase your sense of isolation and maintain your low mood.

✔ **Avoidance behaviours,** such as avoiding situations you perceive as threatening (attending a social outing, using a lift, speaking in public), deprive you of the opportunity to confront and overcome your fears.

Learning Your ABCs

When you start to get an understanding of your emotional difficulties, CBT encourages you to break down a specific problem you have using the *ABC format*, in which:

✔ **A** is the *activating event*. An activating event means a real *external* event that has occurred, a future event that you anticipate occurring or an *internal* event in your mind, such as an image, memory or dream.

The 'A' is often referred to as your 'trigger'.

✔ **B** is your *beliefs*. Your beliefs include your thoughts, your personal rules, the demands you make (on yourself, the world and other people) and the meanings that you attach to external and internal events.

✔ **C** is the *consequences*. Consequences include your emotions, behaviours and physical sensations that accompany different emotions.

Figure 1-1 shows the ABC parts of a problem in picture form.

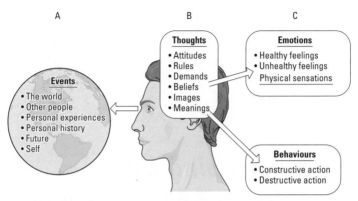

Figure 1-1: A is the activating event, **B** is your beliefs and thoughts, and **C** is the consequences, such as the emotions you feel after the event, and your subsequent behaviour.

Writing down your problem in *ABC form* – a central CBT technique – helps you differentiate between your thoughts, feelings and behaviours, and the *trigger* event. We give more information about the ABC form in Chapter 3.

Consider the ABC formulations of two common emotional problems, anxiety and depression. The ABC of anxiety may look like this:

- ✔ **A:** You imagine failing a job interview.

- ✔ **B:** You believe: 'I've got to make sure that I don't mess up this interview, otherwise I'll prove that I'm a failure.'

- ✔ **C:** You experience anxiety (emotion), butterflies in your stomach (physical sensation), and drinking to calm your nerves (behaviour).

The ABC of depression may look like this:

- ✔ **A:** You fail a job interview.

- ✔ **B:** You believe: 'I should've done better. This means that I'm a failure!'

- ✔ **C:** You experience depression (emotion), loss of appetite (physical sensation), and staying in bed and avoiding the outside world (behaviour).

You can use these examples to guide you when you are filling in an ABC form on your own problems. Doing so will help ensure that you record the actual facts of the event under 'A', your thoughts about the event under 'B', and how you feel and act under 'C'. Developing a really clear ABC of your problem can make it much easier for you to realise how your thoughts at 'B' lead to your emotional/behavioural responses at 'C'. (Chapter 3 describes the ABC form more fully.)

Characterising CBT

Here's a quick reference list of key characteristics of CBT. CBT:

✓ Emphasises the role of the personal meanings that you give to events in determining your emotional responses.

✓ Was developed through extensive scientific evaluation.

✓ Focuses more on how your problems are being *maintained* rather than on searching for a single root cause of the problem.

✓ Offers practical advice and tools for overcoming common emotional problems (see Chapters 9, 12 and 13).

✓ Holds the view that you can change and develop by thinking things through and by trying out new ideas and strategies (head to Chapter 4).

✓ Can address material from your past if doing so can help you to understand and change the way you're thinking and acting now (Chapter 11 covers this in depth).

✓ Shows you that some of the strategies you're using to cope with your emotional problems are actually maintaining those problems (Chapter 6 is all about this).

✓ Strives to normalise your emotions, physical sensations, and thoughts rather than to persuade you that they're clues to 'hidden' problems.

✓ Recognises that you may develop emotional problems *about* your emotional problems, for example feeling ashamed about being depressed (see Chapter 6 for more on this concept).

✓ Highlights learning techniques and maximises self-help so that ultimately you can become your own therapist.

Getting complicated

Sticking to the simple ABC formulation in which A+B=C can serve you well. But if that seems a little simplistic, you can consider the more complicated formulations shown here:

This diagram shows the complex interaction between your thoughts, feelings and behaviours. Although your thoughts affect how you feel, your feelings also affect your thinking. So, if you're having depressed thoughts, your mood is likely to be low. The lower your mood, the more likely you are to act in a depressed manner and to think pessimistically. The combination of feeling depressed, thinking pessimistically and acting in a depressed manner can, ultimately, influence the way you see your personal world. You may focus on negative events in your life and the world in general and therefore accumulate more negative As. This interaction between A, B and C can become a vicious circle.

CBT pays a lot of attention to changing both unhealthy thinking patterns and unhealthy patterns of behaviour.

Chapter 2

Accidental Thinking Mistakes

*Y*ou probably don't spend a lot of time mulling over the pros and cons of the way you think. Most people don't – but to be frank, most people ideally ought to!

One of the central messages of CBT is that the thoughts, attitudes and beliefs you hold have a big effect on the way you interpret the world around you and on how you feel. So, if you're feeling excessively bad, chances are that you're thinking badly – or, at least, in an unhelpful way. Of course, you probably don't *intend* to think in an unhelpful way, and no doubt you're largely unaware that you do.

Thinking errors are slips in thinking that everyone makes from time to time. Just as a virus stops your computer from dealing with information effectively, so thinking errors prevent you from making accurate assessments of your experiences. Thinking errors lead you to get the wrong end of the stick, jump to conclusions and assume the worst. Thinking errors get in the way of, or cause you to distort, the facts. However, you do have the ability to step back and take another look at the way you're thinking and set yourself straight. In this chapter we show you how to do just that.

Months or years after the event, you've probably recalled a painful or embarrassing experience and been struck by how differently you feel about it at this later stage. Perhaps you can even laugh about the situation now. Why didn't you laugh back then? Because of the way you were thinking at the time.

To err is most definitely human. Or, as American psychotherapist Albert Ellis is quoted as saying, 'If the Martians ever find out how human beings think, they'll kill themselves laughing.' By understanding the thinking errors we outline in this chapter, you can spot your unhelpful thoughts and put them straight more quickly. Get ready to identify and respond in healthier ways to some of the most common 'faulty' and unhelpful ways of thinking identified by researchers and clinicians.

Catastrophising: Turning Mountains Back Into Molehills

Catastrophising is taking a relatively minor negative event and imagining all sorts of disasters resulting from that one small event, as we sum up in Figure 2-1.

Figure 2-1: Catastrophising.

Consider these examples of catastrophising:

✔ You're at a party and you accidentally stumble headlong into a flower arrangement. After you extract yourself from the foliage, you scurry home and conclude that everyone at the party witnessed your little trip and laughed at you.

✔ You're waiting for your teenage daughter to return home after an evening at the cinema with friends. The clock strikes 10:00 p.m., and you hear no reassuring rattle of her key in the door. By 10:05 p.m., you start imagining her accepting a lift home from a friend who drives recklessly. At 10:10 p.m., you're convinced she's been involved in a head-on collision and paramedics are at the scene. By 10:15 p.m., you're weeping over her grave.

Catastrophising leads many an unfortunate soul to misinterpret a social faux pas as a social disaster, a late arrival as a car accident or a minor disagreement as total rejection.

Nip catastrophic thinking in the bud by recognising it for what it is – just thoughts. When you find yourself thinking of the worst possible scenario, try the following strategies:

✔ **Put your thoughts in perspective.** Even if everyone at the party did see your flower-arranging act, are you sure no one was sympathetic? Surely you aren't the only person in the world to have tripped over in public. Chances are, people are far less interested in your embarrassing moment than you think. Falling over at a party isn't great, but in the grand scheme of things it's hardly society-page news.

✔ **Consider less terrifying explanations.** What other reasons are there for your daughter being late? Isn't being late for curfew a common feature of adolescence? Perhaps the film ran over, or she got caught up chatting and forgot the time. Don't get so absorbed in extreme emotions that you're startled to find your daughter in the doorway apologising about missing the bus.

✔ **Weigh up the evidence.** Do you have enough information to believe everyone at the party was laughing at you? Look for evidence that contradicts your catastrophic assumption.

> ✓ **Focus on what you can do to cope with the situation, and the people or resources that can come to your aid.** Engaging in a few more social encounters can help you put your party faux pas behind you.

All-or-Nothing Thinking: Finding Somewhere In-between

All-or-nothing or *black-or-white thinking* (see Figure 2-2) is extreme thinking that can lead to extreme emotions and behaviours. People either love you or hate you, right? Something's either perfect or a disaster. You're either responsibility-free or totally to blame? Sound sensible? We hope not!

Figure 2-2: All-or-nothing thinking.

Unfortunately, humans fall into the all-or-nothing trap all too easily:

> ✓ Imagine you're trying to eat healthily in order to lose weight and you cave in to the temptation of a doughnut. All-or-nothing thinking may lead you to conclude that your plan is in ruins and then to go on to eat the other 11 doughnuts in the pack.

> ✓ You're studying a degree course and you fail one module. All-or-nothing thinking makes you decide that the whole

endeavour is pointless. Either you get the course totally right or it's just a write-off.

Consider the humble thermometer as your guide to overcoming the tendency of all-or-nothing thinking. A thermometer reads degrees of temperature, not only 'hot' and 'cold'. Think like a thermometer – in degrees, not extremes. You can use the following pointers to help you change your thinking:

🖊 **Be realistic.** You can't possibly get through life without making mistakes. One doughnut doesn't a diet ruin..

🖊 **Develop 'both–and' reasoning skills.** An alternative to all-or-nothing thinking is *both–and reasoning*. You can *both* succeed in your overall educational goals *and* fail a test or two. Life is not a case of being either a success or a failure.

Fortune-Telling: Stepping Away From the Crystal Ball

Often, clients tell us after they've done something they were anxious about that the actual event wasn't half as bad as they'd predicted. Predictions are the problem here.

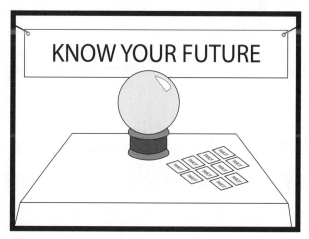

Figure 2-3: Fortune-telling.

✔ You've been feeling a bit depressed lately and you aren't enjoying yourself like you used to. Someone from work invites you to a party, but you decide that if you go you won't have a good time. The other guests are sure to find you boring. So, you opt to stay in and bemoan the state of your social life.

✔ You fancy the bloke who sells you coffee every morning and you'd like to go out with him on a date. You predict that if you ask him, you'll be so anxious that you'll say something stupid. Anyway, he's bound to say no thanks.

You're better off letting the future unfold without trying to guess how it may turn out. Try the following strategies instead:

✔ **Test out your predictions.** You really never know how much fun you might have at a party until you get there. Maybe the chap at the coffee shop will turn you down, but you won't be sure until you ask.

✔ **Be prepared to take risks.** Isn't it worth possibly losing a bit of cash for the opportunity to try a sport you've always been interested in? Learning to live experimentally and taking calculated risks is a recipe for keeping life interesting and rewarding.

✔ **Understand that your past experiences don't determine your future experiences.** Just because the last party you went to turned out to be a dreary homage to the seventies, doesn't mean that you'll never have better luck again.

Typically, fortune-telling stops you from taking action. It can also become a bit of a self-fulfilling prophecy. So, put on your party gear, ask him out for dinner and book yourself in for some hang-gliding.

Mind-Reading: Taking Your Guesses with a Pinch of Salt

So, you think you know what other people are thinking, do you? With *mind-reading* (see Figure 2-4), the tendency is often to assume that others are thinking negative things about you or have negative motives and intentions.

Figure 2-4: Mind-reading.

Here are some examples of mind-reading tendencies:

🖝 You're chatting with someone and they look over your shoulder as you're speaking, break eye contact and (perish the thought) yawn. You conclude immediately that the other person thinks your conversation is mind-numbing and that he'd rather be talking to someone else.

🖝 You pass a neighbour on the street. He says a quick hello but doesn't look very friendly or pleased to see you. You think that he must be annoyed with you about your dog howling at the last full moon and is making plans to report you to environmental health.

You can never know for certain what another person is thinking, so you're wise to pour salt on your negative assumptions. Stand back and take a look at all the evidence to hand. Try the following:

🖝 **Generate some alternative reasons for what you see.** The person you're chatting with may be tired, be preoccupied with his own thoughts or just have spotted someone he knows.

🖝 **Consider that your guesses may be wrong.** Your neighbour was in a hurry to get to the bank and may never have heard your dog anyway.

    ✔ **Get more information.** Ask your neighbour whether your dog kept him up all night, and think of some ways to muffle your pet next time the moon waxes.

Emotional Reasoning: Reminding Yourself That Feelings Aren't Facts

But surely your feelings are real hard evidence of the way things are? Actually, no! Often, relying too heavily on your feelings as a guide leads you off the reality path:

✔ Your partner has been spending long nights at the office with a co-worker for the past month. Based on these feelings, you conclude that your partner's having an affair.

✔ You feel guilty out of the blue. You conclude that you must have done something wrong.

✔ You wake up with a vague sense of dread. You assume that there must be something seriously wrong and search your mind frantically for the source of your ill-feeling.

Often your feelings are simply due to a thought or memory that you may not even be totally aware of having had. As a rule of thumb, it pays to be somewhat sceptical about the validity of your feelings in the first instance.

When you spot emotional reasoning taking over your thoughts, take a step back and try the following:

1. **Take notice of your thoughts.** Take notice of thoughts such as 'I'm feeling nervous, something must be wrong' and 'I'm so angry, and that really shows how badly you've behaved', and recognise that feelings are not always the best measure of reality.

2. **Ask yourself how you'd view the situation if you were feeling calmer.** For example, is there really any evidence that something bad is going to happen?

3. **Give yourself time to allow your feelings to subside.** When you're feeling calmer, review your conclusions

and remember that it is quite possible that your feelings are the consequence of your present emotional state (or even just fatigue) rather than indicators of the state of reality.

4. **If you can't find any obvious and immediate source of your unpleasant feelings – overlook them.** Get into the shower despite your sense of dread, for example. If a concrete reason to be anxious does exist, it won't get dissolved in the shower. If your anxiety is all smoke and mirrors, you may well find it washes down the drain.

Figure 2-5: Emotional reasoning.

Overgeneralising: Avoiding the Part/Whole Error

Overgeneralising is the error of drawing global conclusions from one or more events. When you find yourself thinking 'always', 'never', 'people are . . .' or 'the world's . . .', you may well be overgeneralising. Take a look at Figure 2-6. Here, our stick man sees one black sheep in a flock and instantly assumes wrongly the whole flock of sheep is black.

You might recognise overgeneralising in the following examples:

✔ You feel down. When you get into your car to go to work, it doesn't start. You think to yourself, 'Things like this are always happening to me. Nothing ever goes right', which makes you feel even more gloomy.

✔ You tend to feel guilty easily. You yell at your child for not understanding his homework and then decide that you're a thoroughly rotten parent.

Figure 2-6: Overgeneralising.

Rather than overgeneralising, consider the following:

✔ **Get a little perspective while suspending judgement:** How true is the thought that nothing *ever* goes right for you? How many other people in the world may be having car trouble at this moment?

✔ **Be specific.** Would you be a *totally* rotten parent for losing patience with your child? Perhaps your impatience is simply an area you need to target for improvement.

Making Demands: Thinking Flexibly

Albert Ellis, founder of rational emotive behaviour therapy, one of the first cognitive-behavioural therapies, places demands at the very heart of emotional problems. Thoughts and beliefs that contain words like 'must', 'should', 'need', 'ought', 'got to' and 'have to' are often problematic because they're extreme and rigid (see Figure 2-7).

Consider these possible examples:

✔ You believe that you *must* have the approval of your friends and colleagues. This leads you to feel anxious in many social situations and drives you to try to win everyone's approval – possibly at great personal cost.

✔ You think that because you try very hard to be kind and considerate to others, they really *ought* to be just as kind and considerate in return.

✔ You believe that you *absolutely should* never let people down. At work, you do more than your fair share because you don't assert yourself, and so you often end up feeling stressed and depressed.

Figure 2-7: Demands.

Holding *flexible preferences* about yourself, other people and the world in general is the healthy alternative to inflexible rules and demands. Try the following techniques:

✔ **Pay attention to language.** Replace words like 'must', 'need' and 'should' with 'prefer', 'wish' and 'want'.

✔ **Limit approval seeking.** Can you manage to have a satisfying life even if you don't get the approval of everyone you seek it from?

✔ **Understand that the world doesn't play to your rules.** In fact, other people tend to have their own rulebooks. If you can give others the right to not live up to your standards, you'll feel less hurt when they fail to do so.

✔ **Retain your standards, ideals and preferences, and ditch your rigid demands about how you, others and the world 'have to' be.** So keep acting consistently with how you *would like* things to be rather than becoming depressed or irate about things not being the way you believe they *must* be.

Mental Filtering: Keeping an Open Mind

Mental filtering is a bias in the way you process information, in which you acknowledge only information that fits with a belief you hold. If you think any of the following, you're making the 'mental filtering' thinking error:

✔ You believe you're a failure, so you tend to focus on your mistakes at work and overlook successes and achievements.

✔ You believe you're unlikeable, and *really* notice each time your friend is late to call back or seems too busy to see you.

To combat mental filtering, look more closely at situations you feel down about. Try the following:

✔ **Examine your filters closely.** For example, are you sifting your achievements through an 'I'm a failure' filter? Drop the filter when assessing yourself in the same way you do when looking at your friends' achievements.

✔ **Gather evidence.** Imagine you're collecting evidence for a court case to prove that your negative thought isn't true. What evidence do you cite? Would, for example, an assertion that you're unlikeable stand up in court against the proof of your friends behaving warmly towards you?

Personalising: Removing Yourself from the Centre of the Universe

Personalising involves interpreting events as being related to you personally and overlooking other factors. This can lead to emotional difficulties, such as feeling hurt easily or feeling unnecessarily guilty (see Figure 2-8).

Figure 2-8: Personalising.

Here are some examples of personalising:

- ✔ You may tend to feel guilty if you know a friend is upset and you can't make him feel better. You think, 'If I was really a good friend, I'd be able to cheer him up. I'm obviously letting him down.'

- ✔ You feel hurt when a friend you meet in a shop leaves quickly after saying only a hurried 'hello'. You think, 'He was obviously trying to avoid talking to me. I must have offended him somehow.'

You can tackle personalising by considering alternative explanations that don't revolve around you. Think about the following examples:

> ✔ **Imagine what else may contribute to the outcome you're assuming personal responsibility for.** Your friend may have lost his job or be suffering from depression. Despite your best efforts to cheer him up, these factors are outside your control.

> ✔ **Consider why people may be responding to you in a certain way.** Don't jump to the conclusion that someone's response relates directly to you. For example, your friend may be having a difficult day or be in a big hurry – he may even feel sorry for not stopping to talk to you.

Because you really aren't the centre of the universe, look for explanations of events that have little or nothing to do with you.

Getting intimate with your thinking

Figuring out which thinking errors you tend to make the most can be a useful way of making your CBT self-help more efficient and effective. The simplest way of doing this is to jot down your thoughts whenever you feel upset and note what was happening at the time. Remember the maxim: When you feel bad, put your thoughts on the pad! See Chapter 3 for more on managing unhelpful thoughts by writing them down.

You can then review your thoughts against the list of thinking errors in this chapter. Write down beside each unhelpful thought the specific thinking error you're most probably making. With practice you can get better at spotting your thinking errors and challenging them. In all probability, you may notice that you're more prone to making some errors than others; therefore you know which alternative styles of thinking to develop.

You may also become aware of patterns or themes in the kinds of situations or events that trigger your negative thoughts. These can also help you to focus on the areas in which your thoughts, beliefs and attitudes need most work.

Chapter 3

Tackling Toxic Thoughts

. . . .

In This Chapter

▶ Identifying the thoughts underpinning the way you feel

▶ Questioning your negative thoughts and generating alternatives

▶ Using the ABC self-help form to manage your emotions

. . . .

*1*n your endeavours to become your own CBT therapist, one of the key techniques you use is a tool known as an *ABC form*, which provides you with a structure for identifying, questioning and replacing unhelpful thoughts using pen and paper.

The way you think affects the way you feel. Therefore, changing your unhelpful thoughts is a key to feeling better.

Catching NATs

Getting the hang of the ABC form is often easier if you break down the process into two steps. The first step is to fill out the first three columns (*Activating* event, *Beliefs* and thoughts, *Consequences*) of the form. This gives you a chance to focus on catching your *negative automatic thoughts* (NATs) on paper and to see the connection between your thoughts and emotions.

Using the ABC form is great, but if you don't have one to hand when you feel an upsetting emotion, grab anything you can write on to scribble down your thoughts and feelings. You can always transfer your thoughts to a form later. As has been said by many a CBT therapist: When you feel bad, stick it on the pad!

Making the thought–feeling link

A crucial step in CBT is to make the *thought–feeling link* or *B-to-C connection*; that is, seeing clearly for yourself the connection between what goes through your mind and your resulting emotions. When you see this connection, it can help you to make much more sense of why to challenge and change your thoughts.

Becoming more objective about your thoughts

One of the biggest advantages of writing down your thoughts is that the process can help you to regard these thoughts simply as hunches, theories and ideas – rather than as absolute facts.

The more negative the meaning you give to an event, the more negative you'll feel, and the more likely you'll act in a way that maintains that feeling.

Stepping Through the ABC Form

So, time to embark on this major CBT self-help technique using Figure 3-1. The basic process for completing the ABC form is as follows:

1. **In the 'Consequences' box, point 1, write down the emotion you're feeling.**

   Therapy's about becoming emotionally healthier and acting in a more self-helping or productive way.

   Emotions and behaviour are *consequences* (C) of the interaction between the *activating event or trigger* (A) and the *beliefs or meanings* (B) in the ABC model of emotion.

   Examples of emotions you may choose to list in the 'Consequences' box include:

   • Anger

   • Anxiety

   • Depression

- Envy
- Guilt
- Hurt
- Jealousy
- Shame

Fill out an ABC form when you feel emotionally upset, when you've acted in a way that you want to change, or when you feel like acting in a way that you wish to change.

2. **In the 'Consequences' box, point 2, write down how you acted.**

   Write down how your behaviour changed when you felt your uncomfortable emotion. For example:

   - Avoiding something
   - Becoming withdrawn, isolated or inactive
   - Being aggressive
   - Escaping from a situation
   - Putting off something (procrastination)
   - Seeking reassurance

3. **In the 'Activating Event' box, write down what triggered your feelings.**

   These are the things that triggered your unhelpful thoughts and feelings and can include:

   - Something happening right now
   - Something that occurred in the past
   - Something that you're anticipating happening in the future
   - Something in the external world (an object, place or person)
   - Something in your mind (an image or memory)
   - A physical sensation (increased heart rate, headache, feeling tired)
   - Your own emotions or behaviour

To keep your ABC form brief and accurate, focus on the specific aspect of the activating event that you're upset about. Use the table of emotions in Chapter 5# to help you detect the themes to look out for if you're unsure about what may have triggered your thoughts and feelings.

4. **In the 'Beliefs' box, write down your thoughts, attitudes and beliefs.**

   Describe what the activating event meant to you when you felt the emotion (the 'Consequences').

   The thoughts, attitudes and beliefs you put in the 'Beliefs' box often pop up on reflex. They may be extreme, distorted and unhelpful – but they may *seem* like facts to you. Some examples of these NATs include:

   • Here I go again, proving that I'm useless!

   • I should've known better!

   • Now everyone knows what an idiot I am!

   • This proves that I can't cope like normal people do!

   Thoughts are what count, so think of yourself as a detective and set out to capture suspect thoughts. If your thoughts are in the form of a picture, describe the image, or what the image means to you – then write them down in the 'Beliefs' box.

We think not only in words but also in pictures. People who are feeling anxious frequently describe that they see *catastrophic images* going through their mind. For example, if you fear fainting in a restaurant, you may get an image of yourself on the restaurant floor with staff fussing over you.

5. **In the 'Thinking Error' box, consider what your thinking errors may be.**

   One of the key ways to become more objective about your thoughts is to identify the *thinking errors* that may be represented in the thoughts you list in this box. See Chapter 2.

   Questions that you might ask yourself in order to identify your thinking errors include:

- Am I jumping to the worst possible conclusion? (Catastrophising)

- Am I thinking in extreme – all-or-nothing – terms? (Black-and-white thinking)

- Am I using words like 'always' and 'never' to draw generalised conclusions from a specific event? (Overgeneralising)

- Am I predicting the future instead of waiting to see what happens? (Fortune-telling)

- Am I jumping to conclusions about what other people are thinking of me? (Mind-reading)

- Am I focusing on the negative and overlooking the positive? (Mental filtering)

- Am I globally putting myself down as a failure, worthless or useless? (Labelling)

- Am I listening too much to my negative gut feelings instead of looking at the objective facts? (Emotional reasoning)

- Am I taking an event or someone's behaviour too personally or blaming myself and overlooking other factors? (Personalising)

- Am I using words like 'should', 'must', 'ought' and 'have to' in order to make rigid rules about myself, the world or other people? (Demanding)

Creating Constructive Alternatives

When you feel more confident about identifying your As, Bs, Cs and thinking errors, you can move on to further parts of the ABC form. This helps you question your unhelpful thoughts in order to reduce their intensity, generate and rate the effects of alternative thoughts and focus on acting differently.

Complete the first five steps, then continue with five more steps.

6. **Examine your negative thoughts more closely.**

    Ask yourself the following questions in order to examine and weaken your unhelpful thoughts:

- Can I prove that my thought is 100 per cent true?

- What are the effects of thinking this way?

- Is my thought wholly logical or sensible?

- Do people whose opinions I respect agree that this thought's realistic?

- What evidence exists against this thought?

- Is my thought balanced or extreme?

- Is my thought rigid or flexible?

- Am I thinking objectively and realistically or are my thoughts being biased by how I feel?

 Consider long and hard your negative or unhelpful thoughts in the light of the preceding questions. Don't simply give glib 'yes' or 'no' answers. Instead, think things through and per-haps write down your challenges to your unhelpful thoughts in column D. See the list of questions and prompters at the bottom of the ABC form which can help you further with this.

7. **Generate alternatives for each of your unhelpful thoughts, attitudes and beliefs.**

   This step is critical as it's your alternative thoughts that will help you to feel better! In column D, write down a flexible, non-extreme, realistic and helpful alternative for each thought, attitude or belief that appears in column B. The following questions may help you to generate some alternatives:

   - What's a more helpful way of looking at the situation?

   - Do I encourage friends to think in this way?

   - When I'm feeling okay, how do I think differently?

   - Have any past experiences shown me that another possible outcome exists?

   - What's a more flexible or less extreme way of thinking?

   - What's a more realistic or balanced way of think-ing that takes into account the evidence that does *not* support my thought?

- What do I need to think in order to feel and act differently?

Some thoughts are more stubborn than others, and you won't turn your thinking around completely in one go. Wrestling with NATs for a while before they weaken is typical and appropriate. Think of yourself as *training* your mind to think more flexibly and constructively over a period of time.

8. **In column E, rate the effects of your alternatives on your feelings.**

    Rate your original feelings 0–100 per cent. Also note whether you experience any alternative healthier emotions such as:

    - Concern

    - Annoyance

    - Sadness

    - Remorse

    - Disappointment

    - Sorrow

You won't always notice a great deal of change in how you feel at first, so keep persevering! Changes in the way you behave and think tend to precede improved emotional responses. Keep thinking and acting in line with how you want to ultimately feel.

9. **Develop a plan to move forward.**

    The final step on the ABC form is to develop a plan to move forward. Your plan may be to conduct a behavioural experiment to help you gather more information about whether your thoughts are true or realistic, or to behave differently in a specific situation. Go to Chapters 4 and 5 for more ideas.

Figure 3-2 shows what a typical completed form might look like.

10. **Set yourself some homework.**

    When you've completed several ABC forms, you may well begin to notice recurring themes, thoughts, attitudes or beliefs. Such repetitions may suggest that you need to add some other CBT techniques in order to overcome certain emotions or behaviours, for example:

- Facing a fear until it reduces (Chapter 9)

- Conducting a behavioural experiment to test out a thought (Chapter 4)

- Acting repeatedly 'as if' you believe an alternative thought, attitude or belief (Chapter 17)

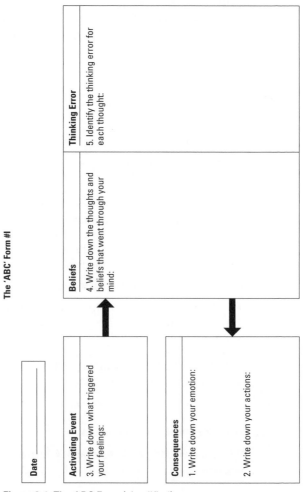

Figure 3-1: The ABC Form (simplified)

The 'ABC' Form #II

Date March 18th

Activating Event (Trigger).	Beliefs, thoughts, and attitudes about A.	Consequences of A+B on your emotions and behaviours.	Dispute (question and examine) B and generate alternatives. The questions at the bottom of the form will help you with this.	Effect of alternative thoughts and beliefs (D).
2. Briefly write down what triggered your emotions. (e.g. event, situation, sensation, memory, image)	3. Write down what went through your mind, or what A meant to you. B's can be about you, others, the world, the past, or the future.	1. Write down what emotion you felt and how you acted when you felt this emotion.	4. Write an alternative for each B, using supporting arguments and evidence.	5. Write down how you feel and wish to act as consequence of your alternatives at D.
Returning to work for the first time after being off sick.	Things will have changed and I won't know what to do (Fortune Telling). People will ask me awkward questions about why I've been off sick and I won't know what to say (Catastrophising). They'll think I'm crazy if they find out I've had depression (Catastrophising, Mind Reading).	**Emotions** e.g. Depression, guilt, hurt, anger, shame, jealousy, envy, anxiety. Rate intensity 0–100. *Anxiety 70%*	*I don't know whether things have changed. Even if they have I've coped with changes many times before. I'm sure my colleagues will help.* *Possibly one or two people will ask, and I can just keep my answers short.* *Mostly everyone will be glad to have me back.*	**Emotions** Re-rate 0–100. List any healthy alternative emotion e.g. Sadness, regret, concern. *Anxiety 40%*
		Behaviour e.g. Avoidance, withdrawing, escape, using alcohol or drugs, seeking reassurance, procrastination *Running over in my mind what I'll say to everyone.*	*I've no reason to think they'll think I'm crazy. When Peter was off with stress people were mostly supportive and understanding. When Helen called last week she seemed to treat me just the same as normal.*	**Alternative Behaviour or Experiment** e.g. Facing situation, increased activity, assertion *Wait and deal with things when I get there, and stop trying to work it out in advance.*

Disputing (Questioning and Examining) and Generating Alternative Thoughts, Attitudes, and Beliefs: 1. Identify your 'thinking errors' at B (e.g. Mind Reading, Catastrophising, Labelling, Demands etc.). Write them next to the appropriate 'B'. 2. Examine whether the evidence at hand supports that your thought at B is 100% true. Consider whether someone whose opinions you respect would totally agree with your conclusions. 3. Evaluate the helpfulness of each B. Write down what you think might be a more helpful, balanced and flexible way of looking at A. Consider what you would advise a friend to think, what a role model of yours might think, or how you might look at A if you were feeling OK. 4. Add evidence and arguments that support your alternative thoughts, attitudes and beliefs. Write as if you were trying to persuade someone you cared about.

Figure 3-2: An example of a filled-in ABC Form.

TIP

Keeping your old ABC forms can be a rewarding record of your progress, and a useful reminder of how to fill them in if you need to use one again in the future. Many of our clients look back over their ABC forms after they feel better and tell us: 'I can't believe I used to feel and think like that!'

An ABC a day keeps the doctor at bay!

If you want to develop any skill, remember these three words: *Practice, practice, practice!* You may not need to fill out an ABC form everyday. Other days, you may need to complete more than one form. The point is that practising ABC forms regularly is worthwhile because:

✔ Practice helps change disturbing feelings and the thoughts that underpin them.

✔ Sinking a new thought into your head and heart takes repetition.

✔ By completing forms on paper, you can become increasingly able to challenge unhelpful thoughts in your head – although you may still need to do it on paper sometimes.

As you progress in your ability to overcome difficulties and develop your CBT self-help skills, you may still find the ABC form useful when you're hit with a biggy. And remember: If you can't work out your unhelpful thinking on the hoof, do sit down and bash it out on paper.

Chapter 4

Behaving like a Scientist: Designing and Conducting Behavioural Experiments

. . . .

In This Chapter

▶ Testing out your thoughts and assumptions as predictions

▶ Exploring theories and gathering information

▶ Designing and recording your experiments

. . . .

*O*ften, CBT can seem like common sense. *Behavioural experiments* are particularly good examples of the common-sense side of CBT. We give you examples of these experiments in action. Try not to home in too much on how the examples differ from your specific problem. Instead, focus on what you have in common with the examples and work from there to apply the techniques to your own problems.

Even in a 'talking treatment' like CBT, actions speak louder than words. Aaron Beck, founder of cognitive therapy, emphasises that testing your thoughts in reality, rather than simply talking about them, underpins effective therapy.

Seeing for Yourself: Reasons for Doing Behavioural Experiments

The proof of the pudding's in the eating. The same can be said of your assumptions, behaviours, beliefs and predictions about yourself and the world around you. Use experiments to test out the *truth* about your beliefs and to assess the *usefulness* of your behaviours.

You can use behavioural experiments in the following ways:

- To test the validity of a thought or belief that you hold about yourself, other people or the world.
- To test the validity of an alternative thought or belief.
- To discover the effects that mental or behavioural activities have on your difficulties.
- To gather evidence in order to clarify the nature of your problem.

Living according to a set of beliefs because you think they're true and helpful is both easy and common. You can also easily stick to familiar ways of behaving because you *think* that they keep you safe from feared events, or that they help you to achieve certain goals. An example of this may be holding a belief that other people are out to find fault with you – with this thought in mind, you then work hard to hide your mistakes and shortcomings.

The beauty of a behavioural experiment is that you may well find that your worst imagined scenarios don't happen, or that you deal with such situations effectively when, or even if, they do occur.

 We may be stating the obvious, but change can be less daunting if you keep in mind that you can always return to your old ways of thinking about things if the new ways don't seem any better. The trick is to prepare yourself to try out new strategies and to give them a chance before returning to your former ways.

Testing Out Predictions

Go through the following four steps to devise a behavioural experiment:

1. **Describe your problem.**

   Write down the nature of your problem and include your *safety behaviours* (things you do to try to prevent your feared catastrophe - see Chapter 5) Phrase the problem in your own words and make a note of how the problem negatively affects your life.

2. **Formulate your prediction.**

Decide what you think will happen if you try out a new way of thinking or behaving in real life.

3. **Execute an experiment.**

Think of a way of putting a new belief or behaviour to the test in a real-life situation. Try to devise more than one way to test out your prediction.

4. **Examine the results.**

Look to see whether your prediction came true. If it didn't, check out what you've learned from the results of the experiment.

You can rate the degree to which you believe a prediction will come true on a percentage between 0 and 100 at the start of your experiment. After you've done the experiment and processed your results, re-rate your conviction in the original prediction.

Take care not to use subtle ways of keeping your feared catastrophe at bay, such as doing experiments only when you feel 'right', are with 'safe' people, have *safety signals* to hand (such as a mobile phone or a bottle of water), or are using safety behaviours (such as trying to control your anxiety with distraction or by gripping tightly to your steering wheel). Using these subtle safety measures during your exposure to a fear can leave you with the impression that you've had a narrow escape, rather than highlighting that your predicted fear didn't come true.

For example, consider the following experiment, which Nadine initiates to examine her fear of rejection and social anxiety:

✔ **Describe the problem.** Nadine's afraid of people thinking negatively of her and of being rejected by her friends. In social situations, Nadine monitors her body language and censors what she says, taking great care not to cause offence. She often plans in advance what she's going to say.

✔ **Formulate a prediction.** Nadine predicts 'If I express an opinion or disagree with my friends, they'll like me less.' She rates her conviction in this idea as 90 per cent.

>   ✔ **Execute an experiment.** For the next six social gather-
>   ings Nadine attends, she decides that she'll speak up and
>   try to offer an opinion. If at all possible, she'll find a point
>   on which to disagree with someone.
>
>   ✔ **Examine the results.** Nadine discovers that no one took
>   exception to her saying more. In fact, two friends com-
>   mented that it was nice to hear more about what she
>   thought about things. Nadine re-rates her conviction in
>   her original prediction as 40 per cent.

By conducting a behavioural experiment, Nadine observed
that her feared prediction – 'Others will like me less if I
express my opinions' – didn't happen. This result gives
Nadine the opportunity to change her behaviour according
to the results of her experiment; therefore, to speak up more
often. It also helps to reduce how much she believes the original prediction. Nadine can now adjust her thinking based on
evidence gathered through the experiment.

Seeking Evidence to See Which Idea Best Fits the Facts

When you want to test out an idea you hold about yourself,
others or the world, try developing an *alternative idea* Some
emotional problems don't respond well to attempts to disprove a negative prediction. In such cases, you may be better
off developing some *competing ideas* about what the problem
actually is. You then devise experiments to gather more evidence and see which idea reflects reality most accurately.

For example, imagine that your boss never says a cheerful
'good morning' to you. You develop the following two ideas:

>   ✔ A: 'My boss doesn't like me at all.'
>
>   ✔ B: 'My boss isn't friendly in the mornings and is a bit
>   rude, but he's like this to a lot of employees, not just me.'

You're now in a position to gather evidence for whether of A
or B best explains the phenomenon of your boss failing to be
cheerful towards you in the mornings.

Often, developing one additional idea to compete with your original one is enough. However, you can develop more ideas if you think they may help you get to the bottom of what you're experiencing. Taking the above example, you may have a third idea, such as 'My boss is cheerful only with employees that he knows very well', or even a fourth idea, such as 'My boss is cheerful only with employees of the same rank or above him'.

Developing competing ideas can be particularly helpful in the following situations:

- ✔ **Dealing with predictions that may be months or years away from being proven.** If you fear you'll go to hell for having an intrusive thought about causing harm to someone, then this outcome is likely to be sometime away. Similarly, if you have *health anxiety* and spend hours each day preoccupied with the idea that physical sensations in your body may be signs that you'll become ill and die, you're unlikely to know straightaway whether this will actually happen. With these kinds of catastrophic thought, you need to design experiments to help you gather evidence that supports the idea that you have a worry or anxiety problem, rather than a damnation or terminal illness.

- ✔ **Dealing with beliefs that are impossible to prove or disprove conclusively.** Perhaps you're anxious about others having negative opinions of you. You cannot know for sure what other people think, but even if someone tells you that your fears are unfounded, you can never know with absolute certainty what he's thinking.

For both of these situations, you can employ the idea A or B strategy:

- ✔ Devise an experiment to test out whether your original idea A that, 'People don't like me', or alternative idea B that, 'I often think that people don't like me because I'm so worried about others' opinions of me that I end up seeing a lot of their behaviour as signs of dislike', best explains your experiences in social situations.

Here is an example of how Alex used the competing theories approach to get a better understanding of his physical sensations. Originally, Alex assumed his idea that uncomfortable bodily sensations signalled the onset of a heart attack was correct. By testing this in practice, Alex was able to consider that an alternative idea – uncomfortable bodily sensations are a by-product of anxiety – may be more accurate.

✔ **Describe the problem.** Alex suffers from panic attacks. He feels hot and his heart races, sometimes out of the blue. When he feels these sensations, he fears he's having a heart attack. Alex sits down to try to reduce the strain on his heart (an example of a safety behaviour). He goes out of his way to avoid situations in which he has experienced these symptoms.

✔ **Develop competing theories.** Alex devises two theories about his raised heart rate:

• Idea A: 'My heart beating quickly means I'm vulnerable to having a heart attack.'

• Idea B: 'My heart beating quickly is a consequence of anxiety.'

✔ **Execute an experiment.** Alex decides to deliberately confront situations that tend to trigger off his raised heart rate and to stay in them, *without sitting down*, until his anxiety reduces. He predicts that if idea B is correct, then his heart rate will reduce after his anxiety subsides and he can leave the situation without having come to any harm.

✔ **Examine the results.** Alex finds that his heart rate does indeed reduce when he stays with his anxiety. He's struck by what a difference this knowledge makes to his confidence, and that he's not going to come to any harm from his raised heart rate when he resists the urge to sit down. He concludes that he can reasonably have about 70 per cent confidence in his new idea that his raised heart rate is a benign consequence of anxiety.

You can't always prove conclusively that something isn't so. However, you can experiment to see whether certain emotional states, and mental or behavioural activities, have a beneficial or detrimental effect on the kinds of thoughts that play on your mind.

Making Observations

Observations can be an easier way of getting started with doing experiments to test out the validity of your thoughts. Observations usually involve collecting evidence related to a specific thought by watching other people in action.

You may assume, for example, that no one in their right mind would admit to not understanding an important point about a work procedure. If they did, they'd no doubt be ridiculed and promptly sacked on the basis of highlighting their incompetence.

Test this assumption by observing what other people actually *do*. Behave like a scientist and gather evidence of others admitting lack of understanding, asking for clarification or owning up to mistakes. Observe whether your prediction that they'll be ridiculed or fired is accurate. Making observations to gather evidence both for and against your assumptions is another way of behaving like a scientist.

Ensuring Successful Behavioural Experiments

To get the highest level of benefit when designing and carrying out behavioural experiments, keep the following in mind:

- ✔ Ensure that the type of experiment you choose is appropriate. Make your experiments challenging enough for you to gain a sense of accomplishment from conducting them. Equally, take care to devise experiments that won't overwhelm you.

- ✔ Have a clear plan about how, when and where (and with whom, if relevant) you plan to carry out your experiment.

- ✔ Be clear and specific about what you want to find out from your experiment – 'to see what happens' is too vague.

- ✔ Decide in advance how you'll know whether your prediction comes true. For example, what are the clues that someone's thinking critically of you?

- ✔ Plan what you'll do if your prediction comes true. For example, how do you respond assertively if someone is actually critical of you?

✔ Use the behavioural experiments record sheet in this chapter to plan and record your experiment.

✔ Consider what obstacles may interrupt your experiment and how you can overcome them.

✔ When evaluating the outcome of your experiment, check that you're not being biased (for example, discounting the positive or mind-reading, thinking errors we describe in Chapter 2) in the way you process your results.

✔ Consider whether you rely on any (including subtle) safety behaviours. Safety behaviours can affect the results of your experiment or determine how confident you feel about the outcome – for example, thinking that you avoided collapsing by concentrating hard, rather than discovering conclusively that your feelings of dizziness are a result of anxiety, not imminent fainting.

✔ Plan ways to consolidate what you discover from your experiment. For example, should you repeat the experiment, devise a new experiment, change your daily activities, or some other action?

Treating your negative and unhelpful thoughts with scepticism is a key to reducing their emotional impact. Experiments can help you to realise that many of your negative thoughts and predictions are not accurate in reality. Therefore, we suggest you take many of your negative thoughts with a pinch or more of salt.

Think about therapy as an experiment, rather than a lifelong commitment, especially at the beginning. By thinking in this manner, you can feel less under pressure and more able to approach therapy with an open mind.

Keeping Records of Your Experiments

All good scientists keep records of their experiments. If you do the same, you can look back over your results in order to:

✔ Draw conclusions.

✔ Decide what kind of experiment you may want to conduct next in order to gather more information.

| ✓ | Remind yourself that many of your negative predictions won't come true.

To help you keep records of your experiments, photocopy Figure 4-1, and use it as often as you like, following the instructions in the figure.

Behavioural Experiment Record Sheet

Date: _____

Prediction or Theory	Experiment	Results	Conclusion/Comments
Outline the thought, belief, or theory you are testing. Rate your strength of conviction 1–100%	Plan what you will do (including where, when, how, with whom), being as specific as you can.	Record what actually happened including relevant thoughts, emotions, physical sensations, and other people's behaviour.	Write down what have you learned about your prediction or theory in light of the results. Re-rate your strength of conviction 0–100%.

Guidance on carrying out a behavioural experiment: 1. Be clear and specific about the negative and alternative predictions you are testing. Rate your strength of conviction in the prediction or theory you are testing or evaluating. 2 Decide upon your experiment, and be as clear as you can be as to how you will measure your results. 3. Record the results of your experiment, emphasizing clear, observable outcomes. 4. Evaluate the results of your experiment. Write down what these results suggest in terms of the accuracy of your predictions, or which theory the evidence supports. 5. Consider whether a further behavioural experiment might be helpful.

Figure 4-1: Photocopy and fill in your own Behavioural Experiment Record Sheet.

Try to have a no-lose perspective on your experiments. If you do one experiment and it goes well, then great! However, if you plan an experiment but ultimately avoid doing it, you can at least identify the thoughts that blocked you. Even if your negative predictions turn out to be accurate, you have an opportunity to see how well you cope – and very probably that it isn't the end of the world – and then decide whether you need to take further action. The point is, you can always gather information that you can make into a useful experience.

Don't take our word for it . . .

This book's full of suggestions on how to reduce and overcome emotional problems. If you're sceptical about whether CBT can work for you, you're in very good company. However, loads of scientific evidence shows that CBT is more effective than all other psychotherapies.

So, CBT may well work for you, but how can you tell? The answer is to consider applying a specific tool or technique for a period of time as an experiment to see how the technique works for you. Depending on the outcome, you can then choose to do more, modify your approach or try something different.

Part II

Charting the Course: Defining Problems and Setting Goals

The 5th Wave   By Rich Tennant

"I've tried Ayurveda, meditation, and aromatherapy but nothing seems to work. I'm still feeling nauseous and disoriented all day."

In this part . . .

*M*ore than a feeling . . . we help you to clearly name your emotions and also help you to work out the difference between helpful and unhelpful emotions. In this part you discover what you want to change in your life, and realise how some of your current solutions to problems may not be benefiting you in the long run. We also offer alternatives to current solutions that may not actually be working for you!

Chapter 5

Exploring Emotions

· ·

· ·

*T*his chapter aims to introduce you to some of the key differences between the unhealthy negative emotions you may experience and their healthy counterparts. The information we offer also helps you to discover ways to identify whether you're experiencing a healthy or an unhealthy emotional response.

You may be wondering why we're focusing on *negative* emotions in this chapter and neglecting positive feelings such as happiness. You may be asking: 'What *is* it with these two? They're so bleak!' The reason for dealing with the negative is that few people pitch up for therapy because they're having problems with positive emotions. Not a lot of people come to us looking for a way to overcome their relentless feelings of contentment. The emotions that give people trouble typically include guilt, anger, depression and shame.

Fortunately, you can *think* what to *feel*, to a greater or lesser extent, which can reduce your emotional discomfort. By choosing to think in healthy and helpful ways, you're more likely to experience healthy emotions.

Naming Your Feelings

If someone asks you how you feel, you may have difficulty describing exactly which emotion you're feeling. You may not be sure what name to give to your internal experience, or perhaps you're feeling more than one emotion at the same time.

Don't get caught up on words! When you start to make a distinction between healthy and unhealthy feelings, what you call them isn't terribly important. Some people find it simpler to choose a descriptive word for their emotion and to add the term 'healthy' or 'unhealthy' to that word. I

The following is a reference list of common human emotions and their synonyms:

- **Angry:** aggressive, annoyed, bad-tempered, complaining, confounded, cross, displeased, enraged, fractious, fuming, furious.

- **Anxious:** agitated, apprehensive, fearful, fretful, frightened, jumpy, nervous, worried.

- **Ashamed:** belittled, disgraced, dishonoured, humiliated, mortified.

- **Disappointed:** crestfallen, deflated, dejected, discouraged, gutted.

- **Embarrassed:** awkward, diminished, humiliated, ill at ease, self-conscious, unconfident, unsure of oneself.

- **Envious:** green with envy, malevolent, malicious, Schadenfreude, sour, spiteful.

- **Guilty:** at fault, blameworthy, condemned, culpable, deplorable, indefensible, inexcusable, in the wrong.

- **Hurt:** aggrieved, broken-hearted, cut to the quick, cut up, damaged, devastated, gutted, harmed, wounded.

- **Jealous:** bitter and twisted, distrustful, doubtful, green-eyed, sceptical, suspicious, wary.

- **LOVE:** (we threw this one in just to lighten the mood) admiring, adoring, affectionate, besotted, blissful, crazed, devoted, enamoured, esteemed, fond, head over heels, infatuated, keen, loved-up, love-struck, mad about, on cloud nine, smitten, struck by cupid's arrow.

✔ **Sad:** bereft, blue, depressed, distraught, distressed, down, melancholic, mournful, shattered, sorrowful, tearful.

Thinking What to Feel

One benefit of understanding the difference between healthy and unhealthy emotions is that you give yourself a better chance to check out what you're thinking. If you recognise that you're experiencing an unhealthy emotion, you're then in a position to challenge any faulty thinking that may be leading to your unhealthy emotional response. Disputing and correcting thinking errors can help you to experience a healthy, negative emotion instead of an unhealthy feeling.

A common axiom is 'I think therefore I am'; a CBT version is 'I think; therefore I feel.'

Understanding the Anatomy of Emotions

Figure 5-1 shows the complex processes involved in human emotion. Whenever you feel a certain emotion, a whole system is activated. This system includes the thoughts and images that enter your mind, the memories you access, the aspects of yourself or the surrounding world that you focus on, the bodily and mental sensations you experience, physical changes such as appetite, your behaviour, and the things you *feel like* doing.

As the diagram shows, these different dimensions interact in complex ways. For example, training your attention on possible threats is likely to increase the chance of anxious thoughts popping into your mind, and vice versa. Not sleeping well may increase the chances of you being inactive; continued inactivity can further disrupt your usual sleeping pattern. The advantage of understanding this system of emotion as presented in Figure 5-1 is that it gives you plenty of opportunity to make changes. Changing even one aspect of the system can make changing other parts easier.

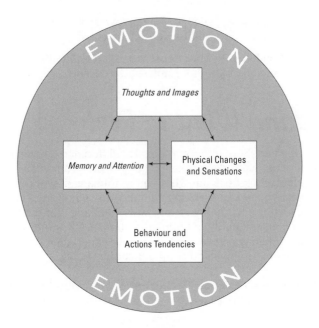

Figure 5-1: The anatomy of emotion.

Comparing Healthy and Unhealthy Emotions

Deciphering between healthy and unhealthy versions of negative emotions can be challenging, especially when the process is new to you. Think of Table 5-1 as your emotional ready reckoner for the characteristics of both healthy and unhealthy emotions. Everything you may need to identify the emotion you're experiencing is in this table. Plus, if you do identify that an emotion you're experiencing is unhealthy, you can implement the thoughts, attention focuses and behaviours of the healthy version to aid you in feeling better.

Table 5-1		Healthy and Unhealthy Emotions		
Emotion	*Theme*	*Thoughts*	*Attention Focus*	*Behaviour/Action Tendencies*
Anxiety (unhealthy)	Threat or danger	Has rigid or extreme attitudes	Monitors threat or danger excessively	Withdraws physically and mentally from threats
		Over-estimates degree of threat		Uses superstitious behaviour to ward off threat
		Under-estimates ability to cope with threat		Numbs anxiety with drugs or alcohol
		Increases threat-related thoughts		Seeks reassurance
Concern (healthy)	Threat or danger	Has flexible and preferential attitudes	Doesn't see threat where no threat exists	Faces up to threat
		Views threat realistically		Deals with threat constructively
		Realistically assesses ability to cope with threat		Doesn't seek unneeded reassurance
		Doesn't increase threat-related thoughts		

(continued)

Table 5-1 (continued)

Emotion	Theme	Thoughts	Attention Focus	Behaviour/Action Tendencies
Depression (unhealthy)	Loss or failure	Has rigid and extreme attitudes	Dwells on past loss/failure	Withdraws from others
		Sees only negative aspects of loss/failure		
	Ruminates on unsolvable problems	Neglects self and living environment		
		Feels helpless	Focuses on personal flaws and failings	Attempts to end feelings of depression in self-destructive ways
		Thinks future is bleak and hopeless	Focuses on negative world events	
Sadness (healthy)	Loss or failure	Has flexible and preferential attitudes	Doesn't dwell on past loss/failure	Talks to significant others about feelings about loss/failure
		Sees both negative and positive aspects of loss/failure	Focuses on problems that one can change	Continues to care for self and living environment
		Is able to help self	Focuses on personal strengths and skills	Avoids self-destructive behaviours

Emotion	Theme	Thoughts	Attention Focus	Behaviour/Action Tendencies
		Is able to think about future with hope	Balances focus between positive and negative world events	
Anger (unhealthy)	Personal rule is broken or self-esteem is threatened	Has rigid and extreme attitudes	Looks for evidence of malicious intent in other person	Seeks revenge
		Assumes other person acted deliberately	Looks for evidence of offensive behaviour being repeated by other people	Attacks other person physically or verbally
		Thinks of self as right and other person as wrong		Takes anger out on innocent person, animal or object
		Cannot see other person's point of view		Withdraws aggressively/sulks
				Recruits allies against other person

(continued)

Table 5-1 (continued)

Emotion	Theme	Thoughts	Attention Focus	Behaviour/Action Tendencies
Annoyance (healthy)	Personal rule broken or self-esteem is threatened	Has flexible and preferential attitudes	Looks for evidence that other person may not have malicious intent	Doesn't seek revenge
		Considers other person may not have acted deliberately	Doesn't see further offence where it may not exist	Asserts self without physical/verbal violence
		Considers that both self and other person may be right to some degree		Doesn't take out feelings on innocent parties
		Is able to see other person's point of view		Remains in situation, striving for resolution (doesn't sulk)
				Requests other person to change their offensive behaviour
Shame (unhealthy)	Shameful personal information has been publicly revealed by self or others	Over-estimates shamefulness of information revealed	Sees disapproval from others where it doesn't exist	Hides from others to avoid disapproval

Emotion	Theme	Thoughts	Attention Focus	Behaviour/Action Tendencies
		Over-estimates degree of dis-approval from others		May attack others who have shamed self, in attempt to save face
		Over-estimates how long dis-approval will last		May try to repair self-esteem in self-destructive ways
				Ignores attempts from social group to return to normal
Regret (healthy)	Shameful personal information has been publicly revealed by self or others	Is compassionately self-accepting about information revealed	Focuses on evidence that self is accepted by social group despite information revealed	Continues to participate in social interaction
		Is realistic about degree of disapproval from others		Responds to attempts from social group to return to normal
		Is realistic about how long disapproval will last		

(continued)

Table 5-1 (continued)

Emotion	Theme	Thoughts	Attention Focus	Behaviour/Action Tendencies
Hurt (unhealthy)	Other person treats one badly (self is undeserving)	Has rigid and extreme attitudes	Looks for evidence of other person not caring or being indifferent	Stops communicating with other person/sulks
		Over-estimates unfairness of other's behaviour		Punishes other person through silence or criticism, without stating what one feels hurt about
		Thinks other person doesn't care		
		Thinks of self as alone and uncared for		
		Dwells on past hurts		
		Thinks other person must make first move towards resolution		
Disappoint-ment (healthy)	Other person treats one badly (self is undeserving)	Has flexible and preferential attitudes	Focuses on evidence that other person does care and isn't indifferent	Communicates with other person about feelings
		Is realistic about degree of unfairness of other's behaviour		Tries to influence other person to act in fairer manner

Emotion	Theme	Thoughts	Attention Focus	Behaviour/Action Tendencies
		Thinks other person acted badly but doesn't think that they don't care		
		Doesn't think of self as alone or uncared for		
		Doesn't dwell on past hurts		
		Doesn't wait for other person to make first move		
Jealousy (unhealthy)	Threat to relationship with partner from another person	Has rigid and extreme attitudes	Looks for sexual/romantic connotations in partner's conversations with others	Seeks constant reassurance that partner is faithful and loving
		Over-estimates threat to the relationship	Creates visual images of partner being unfaithful	Monitors and/or restricts partner's movements and actions
		Thinks partner is always on verge of leaving for another	Looks for evidence that partner is having an affair	Retaliates for partner's imagined infidelity

(continued)

Table 5-1 (continued)

Emotion	Theme	Thoughts	Attention Focus	Behaviour/Action Tendencies
		Thinks partner will leave for another person who they have admitted to finding attractive		Sets tests/traps for partner
				Sulks
Concern for relationship (healthy)	Threat to relationship with partner from another person	Has flexible and preferential attitudes	Doesn't look for evidence that partner is having an affair	Allows partner to express love without needing excessive reassurance
		Is realistic about degree of threat to relationship	Doesn't create images of partner being unfaithful	Allows partner freedom without monitoring them
		Thinks partner finding others attractive is normal	Views partner's conversation with others as normal	Allows partner to express natural interest in opposite sex without imagining infidelity
Unhealthy envy (unhealthy)	Another person possesses something desirable (self lacks desired thing)	Has rigid and extreme attitudes	Focuses on how to get the desired possession without regard for any consequences	Criticises the person with desired possession

Emotion	Theme	Thoughts	Attention Focus	Behaviour/Action Tendencies
		Thinks about the desired possession in a negative way to try to reduce its desirability	Focuses on how to deprive other person of the desired possession	Criticises the desired possession
		Pretends to self that one is happy without desired possession even though this is untrue		Attempts to steal/destroy the desired possession in order to deprive others
Guilt (unhealthy)	Broken moral code (by failing to do something or by committing a sin), hurting or offending significant other	Has rigid and extreme attitudes	Looks for evidence of others blaming one for the sin	Desires to escape from guilt feelings in self-defeating ways
		Thinks one has definitely sinned	Looks for evidence of punishment or retribution	Begs for forgiveness

(continued)

Table 5-1 (continued)

Emotion	Theme	Thoughts	Attention Focus	Behaviour/Action Tendencies
		Thinks that one deserves punishment		Promises that a sin will never be committed again
		Ignores mitigating factors		Punishes self either physically or through deprivation
		Ignores other people's potential responsibility for sin		Attempts to disclaim any legitimate responsibility for the wrongdoing as an attempt to alleviate feelings of guilt
Remorse (healthy)	Broken moral code (by failing to do something or by committing a sin), hurting or offending significant other	Has flexible and preferential attitudes	Doesn't look for evidence of others blaming oneself for the sin	Faces up to healthy pain that comes with knowing that one has sinned

Emotion	Theme	Thoughts	Attention Focus	Behaviour/Action Tendencies
		Considers actions in context and with understanding before making a judgement about whether one has sinned	Doesn't look for evidence of punishment or retribution	Asks for forgiveness
		Takes appropriate level of responsibility for the sin		Atones for the sin by taking a penalty and/or making appropriate amends
		Considers mitigating factors		Doesn't have tendency to be defensive or to make excuses for the poor behaviour
		Doesn't believe that punishment is deserved and/or imminent		

Themes refer to situational aspects linked to emotion. Themes are the same for both healthy and unhealthy negative emotions. For example, when you feel *guilty* (an unhealthy negative emotion), the theme for that emotion is that you've 'sinned' by either *doing* or *failing to do* something. Another way of saying that you're guilty is that you've transgressed or failed to live up to your moral code. *Remorse*, the healthy alternative to guilt, results from the same theme as guilt. However, your thoughts, behaviours and focus of attention are different when you are remorseful and when you are guilty.

Themes can be useful in helping you to put your finger on the nature of the emotion you're experiencing. However, themes are not enough to help you decide whether your emotion is a healthy or unhealthy one. Consider the following situation:

> Imagine that you have an elderly aunt who needs your help to continue living independently. You usually visit her at the weekend and do jobs that she's too frail to do for herself, like changing light bulbs and cleaning windows. Last weekend you went skiing with friends instead of checking in on your aunt. She became impatient waiting for the light bulb in her hallway to be changed and tried to do it herself. Unfortunately, your aunt fell off the chair she was standing on and broke her hip.

Thematically, this situation is one in which you broke or failed to fulfil a personal moral code, resulting in hurting or offending someone else.

If you feel guilty (an unhealthy negative emotion), you're very likely to experience the following:

- ✔ **Type of thinking:** Your thinking becomes rigid and demand-based. You conclude that you've definitely done a bad thing (sinned). You assume more personal responsibility than may actually be legitimate, discounting or not considering mitigating factors. You may believe that some form of punishment is deserved and/or imminent.

- ✔ **Focus of attention:** You look for more evidence that you've sinned, or you look for evidence that others hold you responsible for the sin.

🖝 **Behaviour (action tendency):** You may desire to escape from guilty feelings in self-defeating ways – for example, begging for forgiveness, promising that you'll never commit a sin again, punishing yourself, physically or through deprivation, or by attempting to disclaim any legitimate responsibility for the wrongdoing.

Action tendency refers to an urge for you to behave in a certain way that you may or may not actually act upon. Different emotions produce an urge within you to do certain things. In some cases, you may actually do or say something, and in others you may just be aware that you *want* to do or say something; for example, *wanting* to run out of a room and hide when feeling ashamed, or feeling unhealthily angry and *wanting* to punch someone's lights out, without actually doing so. By contrast, you can think about the situation differently and feel remorse (a healthy negative emotion). Although the same theme (a broken or failed moral code, causing hurt or offence to a significant other) still applies, you experience the following:

🖝 **Type of thinking:** Your thinking is more flexible and preference-based. You look at actions in context and with understanding before making a judgement about whether you sinned. You consider mitigating factors of the situation and do not believe that punishment is deserved and/ or imminent.

🖝 **Focus of attention:** You don't look for further evidence that you sinned. Neither do you look for evidence that others hold you responsible for the sin.

🖝 **Behaviour (action tendency):** You face up to the healthy pain that comes with knowing that you've sinned. You may ask for, but not beg for, forgiveness. You understand the reasons for your wrongdoing and act on that understanding. You may atone for the sin by taking a penalty and/or making appropriate amends. You avoid defensiveness and excuse-making.

The theme involving both guilt and remorse is the same, but your thinking, action tendencies and focus of attention are very different.

Spotting the difference in thinking

As the example in the preceding section illustrates, unhealthy emotions can spring from rigid, *demand-based thinking.* Thoughts or beliefs like 'other people must behave respectfully towards me at all times' and 'I should always get what I want without hassle' can lead to unhealthy anger when other people and the world don't meet these demands.

Healthy emotions spring from flexible, *preference-based thinking.* So, thoughts and beliefs like 'I prefer others to treat me respectfully, but they're not bound to do so' and 'I prefer to get what I want without hassle, but no reason exists that this should always be the case' can lead to healthy annoyance when other people and the world don't meet your preferences.

Rigid thinking is a reliable indicator that you're having an unhealthy feeling. When you think rigidly, you're more likely to underestimate your ability to cope with and overcome the negative event in question. The more adept you become at identifying your thoughts, beliefs and attitudes as either rigid and demanding or flexible and preferential, the easier you can work out whether your feelings are healthy or unhealthy.

When you feel *guilty*, you think in an unhealthy, rigid, demand-based manner and may say things like the following:

- ✔ 'I absolutely shouldn't have left my aunt alone.'

- ✔ 'Leaving my aunt alone was a bad thing and means I'm a bad person.'

- ✔ 'I can't bear the pain of knowing that I've done this bad thing of leaving my aunt alone.'

You may then continue to think in the following guilt-enhancing ways:

- ✔ You fail to acknowledge that your aunt ultimately chose to try to change the light bulb herself. You fail to acknowledge that other members of your family can also check in on your aunt.

✔ You ignore the fact that you had no way of knowing that the light bulb needed changing, and that you had not foreseen your aunt taking such a risk.

✔ You expect that your aunt will blame your entirely. You think about the punishment that you believe you deserve.

By contrast, if you feel *remorseful*, you think in a healthy, flexible, preference-based manner and may say things such as:

✔ 'I wish I hadn't left my aunt alone, but regrettably I did.'

✔ 'Leaving my aunt alone may mean that I've done a bad thing but not that I'm a bad person.'

✔ 'I can bear the pain of knowing that I've done this bad thing of leaving my aunt alone.'

You can then continue to think in helpful ways:

✔ You can acknowledge your part in the accident occurring, but you can also consider that other members of the family failed to check in on your aunt.

✔ You can acknowledge that you didn't foresee your aunt taking the risk of changing a light bulb. Nor did you know that the bulb would burn out.

✔ You can expect that your aunt may be upset with you, but you believe that you don't deserve a severe punishment.

Taking legitimate responsibility for what happens in a situation enables you to think about the event in a holistic way. You don't need to prolong uncomfortable feelings of remorse beyond what is reasonable and appropriate to the situation. Your ability to solve problems isn't impeded by feelings of guilt.

Spotting the difference in behaving, and ways you want to behave

Another way of figuring out whether your emotion is in the healthy or unhealthy camp is to have a look at your actual behaviour or the way in which you feel inclined to behave.

Healthy negative emotions are accompanied by largely constructive behaviours, whereas unhealthy feelings usually go hand-in-hand with self-defeating behaviours. Problem-solving is still possible when you're healthily sad, annoyed, remorseful or regretful, but you have much greater difficulty planning clear ways to surmount your problems when you're unhealthily depressed, enraged, guilty or ashamed.

For example, if you respond to your aunt's falling over with *guilt-based action tendencies*, you may do one or more of the following:

✔ Go out and get quite drunk, trying to block out your guilty feelings.

✔ Visit your aunt in hospital and plead for her forgiveness.

✔ Promise that you'll never again let down your aunt, or anyone else dear to you, for as long as you live.

✔ Decide that you won't go on any other trips while your aunt is alive.

The preceding behaviours are problematic because they're extreme and unrealistic. These actions focus on self-punishment rather than look at the reality of the situation and how you can, in this example, best meet your aunt's needs.

On the other hand, if you're feeling healthy remorse your *action tendencies* may include some of the following:

✔ Endure the discomfort of knowing that your aunt has been hurt (rather than getting drunk to avoid it).

✔ Visit your aunt in hospital regularly and apologise for having left her alone.

✔ Understand that your aunt needs continuous support but that you have the right to go away with friends.

✔ Plan to stay with your aunt for a week or so after she's discharged from hospital.

✔ Resolve to plan your trips away more carefully and to arrange for nursing staff to be with your aunt when you're unavailable.

The preceding behaviours are geared towards making sure that your aunt doesn't hurt herself again during your absence. By taking an appropriate amount of responsibility for the accident, you can still look for ways to provide comfort for your aunt rather than concentrate on punishing yourself.

Spotting the difference in what you focus on

In addition to differences in types of thinking and behaving, you can distinguish healthy from unhealthy emotions by checking out the focus of your attention. If you're having an unhealthy emotion, your mind is likely to focus on catastrophic possibilities in the future based on the primary event.

If you're responding to the injured auntie situation from a place of *guilt*, you may focus your attention on the following:

✔ Blaming yourself for abandoning your aunt and for the accident happening.

✔ Feeling the pain of your guilt whilst neglecting to consider potential solutions to the problem of your aunt needing continuous care.

✔ Looking for evidence that your aunt blames you entirely for the accident.

✔ Looking for blame from other people, such as hospital staff and family members.

You continue to give yourself an unduly rough ride, thereby prolonging your distressing, guilt feelings by focusing on the bleakest possible aspects of your aunt's accident.

If you respond to the situation from a place of remorse, you are likely to focus your attention on the following:

✔ Accepting that leaving your aunt alone may have been a bad decision but that you had no intention of putting her at risk.

✔ Feeling the pain of remorse over the accident but also trying to find ways to improve the situation.

✔ Not seeking out evidence of blame from your aunt.

✔ Accepting evidence that hospital staff or family members do not blame you for the accident.

Thus, your attention focus when you respond from a place of remorse enables you to take some responsibility for your aunt's broken hip, but you don't dwell on the potential for blame and punishment.

Spotting Similarities in Your Physical Sensations

Butterflies in your stomach, blood racing through your veins, light-headedness, sweaty palms, heart pounding. Sound familiar? We expect so. If someone described these physical symptoms to you, you may try to guess what emotion they were experiencing. However, it would be difficult to confidently determine the specific emotion, because these sensations can accompany several different positive and negative emotional states. For example, you may get butterflies in your stomach when you're excited, angry, anxious or in love, as illustrated in Figure 5-2.

Figure 5-2: Spot the similarities in your physical sensations.

The sensations that you feel in your body also tend to over-lap in both healthy and unhealthy negative emotions. For example, you may get butterflies in your stomach when you're unhealthily anxious *and* when you're healthily concerned. Therefore, using your physical symptoms as a guide to judging the healthiness of your negative feelings isn't very reliable.

The main way in which your physical responses are likely to vary between the healthy and unhealthy categories is in their intensity. You probably find that sensations are more intense, uncomfortable and debilitating when you're having unhealthy emotions, such as anxiety and anger. You may also notice that uncomfortable physical sensations last longer when you're experiencing unhealthy negative emotions.

Incidentally, we believe that if you're experiencing butterflies, sweaty palms, racing blood, light-headedness and a pounding heart all at once, then you really *are* in love!

Identifying Feelings about Feelings

Getting two emotions for the price of one isn't such a great deal when two unhealthy negative emotions are on offer.

Sometimes, you can give yourself a second helping of unhealthy emotion by holding rigid demands about which emotions you believe are acceptable for you to experience in the first place.

A common example of feelings about feelings is found in depression. Many people have guilty feelings about their depression. This guilt often comes from the demands people make of themselves, for example that they mustn't let other people down or put undue strain on loved ones. Here are some typical guilt-producing thoughts that are common in depressed people:

> ✔ 'I should be contributing more to the running of the home.'
>
> ✔ 'I must be able to demonstrate love and care to my children.'
>
> ✔ 'My partner and children are worried about me, and I'm making them suffer.'
>
> ✔ 'I shouldn't be neglecting my friends in this way.'

Recognising your meta-emotions is important, because meta-emotions can prevent you from dealing with your primary emotional problems. For example, you may be feeling guilty about having depression. If you can stop feeling guilty, you'll almost certainly find that you can work on overcoming your depression more effectively.

If you find that the concept of feeling guilty about being depressed really does strike a chord with you, go to Chapter 9, where we discuss it in more detail.

Handy emotional health checklist

The following is an abbreviated list of ways that can help you to find out the nature of a feeling and give it a name. The list can also help you assess whether an emotion is of the healthy or unhealthy negative variety.

✔ Have you identified a word to describe how you feel inside?

✔ Can you identify the theme of your emotion?

✔ How does your emotion lead you to behave? Are your actions or urges to act helpful or unhelpful?

✔ Are you thinking in a flexible way, or are you thinking in a rigid and demanding way?

✔ What are you paying attention to? Are you looking at the event from all angles?

✔ Is another emotion getting in the way of you being able to identify your first emotion? For example, are you feeling guilty or ashamed about your anger, depression or other emotion?

Defining Your Emotional Problems

The aim of CBT is to help you overcome your emotional problems and move you towards your goals. As with all kinds of problem-solving, *defining* your emotional problems is the first step in solving those problems.

Making a statement

Writing down a problem statement has three main components – the emotion, the theme or event (what you feel your emotion about), and what you do in response to that emotion. You can effectively describe an emotional problem by filling in the blanks of the following statement:

Feeling_____ (emotion) about
_____ (theme or event), leading me
to_____ (response).

For example:

Feeling *anxious* about *my face turning red in social situations*, leading me to *avoid going out to bars and clubs and to splash my face with water if I feel hot.*

Feeling *depressed* about *the end of my relationship with my girlfriend, leading me to spend too much time in bed, avoid seeing people and take less care of myself.*

Rating your emotional problem

Human nature leads you to focus on how bad you feel, rather than how much better you feel. As you reduce the intensity of any emotional disturbance, you can find motivation in being able to see a difference. After you describe a problematic emotion, rate it on a scale of 0–10, based on how much distress the emotion causes you and how much it interferes with your life.

As you work on resolving your emotional problem by making changes to your thinking and behaviour, continue to rate the distress and interference it is causing you. Your ratings are likely to go down over time as you make efforts to overcome your unhealthy negative emotions. Review your ratings regularly, once a week or so. Doing this review helps remind you of your progress and replenishes your motivation to keep up the good work!

Share your ratings with your CBT therapist if you have one. Your therapist can haul out your rating records and show you the progress you've made if your motivation begins to flag.

Chapter 6

Identifying Solutions That Cause You Problems

● ●

In This Chapter

▶ Understanding how common coping strategies can maintain (and worsen) your problems

▶ Examining and eliminating safety behaviours

▶ Understanding why doing the opposite of your current strategies can help you

● ●

*T*he first step in any kind of problem-solving is to *define* the problem. This chapter is about assessing your problems and putting your finger on the way in which your current coping strategies are part of your specific problem.

Often, the problematic behaviours that maintain or worsen emotional problems are the very behaviours that people use to help themselves cope – hence the common CBT expression 'your solution is the problem'.

The reality is that you probably weren't taught how to best tackle emotional problems such as anxiety, depression and obsessions. We confess that even though we've been trained in the art of emotional problem-solving, when it comes to dealing with our own emotions, we can still manage to get it wrong.

In this chapter, we guide you towards identifying the fact that your coping strategies may make you feel better in the short term but that they're actually counterproductive – and that they can make things worse in the long term.

When Feeling Better Can Make Your Problems Worse

Aaron Beck, founder of CBT and Dennis Greenberger, a well-known CBT therapist, note that, if you can turn a counterproductive strategy on its head, you're well on the way to a real solution. This concept basically means that by doing the complete opposite of your established coping strategies you can recover from your problems. Exposing yourself to feared situations rather than avoiding them is a good example of turning a counterproductive strategy on its head. The more you avoid situations that you fear, the more afraid you become of ever encountering feared situations. Avoidance also undermines your sense of being able to cope with unpleasant or uncomfortable events. For example, never using a lift may temporarily stop your anxious feelings about being in an enclosed space, but avoiding lifts does not help you to overcome your fear of enclosed spaces once and for all.

Windy Dryden, who trained us in CBT, coined the phrase 'Feel better, get worse; feel worse, get better' when referring to people overcoming emotional problems. Many of the things that you may be doing – but in so doing maintaining your current problems – are driven by a highly understandable goal to reduce your distress. However, when you aim to get short-term relief, you may well be reinforcing the very beliefs and behaviours that underpin your problems.

One of the most powerful ways of changing your emotions in a lasting way, is to act against your unhelpful beliefs and to act on your alternative helpful beliefs (Chapters 3 and 11 contain more information about forming alternative healthy beliefs).

Here are some further examples of what we mean by *problem-maintaining solutions*:

- ✔ **Avoiding situations that you fear or that provoke anxiety.** Avoidance tends to erode rather than boost your confidence. You remain afraid of the situations you avoid, thus you don't give yourself a chance to confront and overcome your fears.

- ✔ **Drinking alcohol or taking drugs to block out uncomfortable feelings.** Often, those bad feelings persist in the long term, and you end up with the added problem of the effect of the alcohol or drugs (hangover, comedown).

✔ **Concealing aspects of yourself that cause you shame.** Hiding things about yourself – such as imperfections in your appearance, childhood experiences, mistakes from the past or current psychological difficulties – can make you feel chronically insecure that someone may 'find you out'. Hiding shameful aspects of your experiences also denies you the opportunity to find out that other people have similar experiences, and that they won't think any less of you for revealing your secrets.

✔ **Putting off dealing with problems or tasks until you're in the mood.** If you wait to take action until 'the right time', until you 'feel like it' or when you feel sufficiently inspired, you may wait a very long time. Putting off essential tasks may save you some discomfort in the short term, but undone tasks also tend to weigh heavily on your mind.

The following sections deal with common counterproductive strategies for coping with common psychological problems. We explain that doing what makes you feel briefly better may be perpetuating your problem.

Getting Over Depression without Getting Yourself Down

If you're feeling depressed, you're likely to be less active and may withdraw from social contact. Inactivity and social withdrawal are often attempts to cope with depressed feelings, but they can reduce the positive reinforcement you get from life, increase isolation, increase fatigue, lead to the build-up of problems or chores, and leave you feeling guilty.

For example, if you've been feeling depressed for some time, you may use a number of ultimately negative strategies to relieve your depression:

✔ To avoid feeling ashamed about being depressed, you may avoid seeing friends. This coping strategy leaves you feeling more isolated and means you don't get the support you need.

✔ To avoid being irritable around your partner or children, you may try to minimise contact with them. Your children may become unruly, your relationship with your partner may suffer, and you may end up feeling guilty about not spending time with any of them.

✔ To avoid the embarrassment of making mistakes at work, you may stop going to work on a regular basis.

✔ To cope with feeling tired and to get some relief from your depression, you may take naps during the day. Unfortunately, napping can disrupt your sleeping pattern, leading to even more fatigue.

To see how your depression is affecting your activity levels, record a typical week on the *activity schedule* in Chapter 9. Then, as we explain in Chapter 9, combat depression by scheduling your activities and rest periods (but not naps because napping during the day can disrupt night time sleeping) for each day, and gradually build up your activity levels over time.

Certainty in an Uncertain World

The need for certainty is a common contributing factor in anxiety, obsessional problems and jealousy.

Unfortunately, the only things you can be 100 per cent sure of, as the saying goes, are birth, death and taxes. Over and above that, humans live in a pretty uncertain universe. Of course, many things are predictable and pretty sure bets, like the sun rising in the morning and setting in the evening. However, other things in life are much more uncertain. 'Will I be pretty?' 'Will I be rich?' 'Will I live to a ripe old age surrounded by grandchildren and a few cats?' *Qué será, será*. Whatever will be, will be.

Trying to get rid of doubt by seeking unattainable certainty is like trying to put out a fire by throwing more wood on it. If you're intolerant of uncertainty, as soon as you quell one doubt another one's sure to pop up. The trick is to find ways to tolerate doubt and uncertainty – they exist whether you like it or not. Here are some examples of how your demands for certainty may be reflected in your behaviour:

✔ **Frequent requests for reassurance.** Constantly asking yourself and other people questions, such 'Do you find that person more attractive than me?', 'Are you sure I haven't gained weight?', 'Do you think I'll pass the exam?' or 'Are you sure I won't get mugged if I go out?' are all efforts to find some reassurance in an uncertain world. Unfortunately, excessive reassurance-seeking can reduce your confidence in your own judgement.

✔ **Repeated checking behaviours.** Checking behaviours are actions you perform in an effort to create more certainty in your world. Such actions include checking several times that your doors and windows are locked, frequently asking your partner where they've been, seeing lots of different doctors to ensure that a physical sensation isn't a sign of serious illness, checking that you can still feel your hip bones and not fat, and going over conversations in your mind to be sure that you haven't said anything offensive. The irony is that the more you check, the more uncertain you feel. You may feel temporarily better immediately following your checks, but it's not long before you feel compelled to carry them out again. Excessive checking can be very time-consuming and tiring, and it can lower your mood.

✔ **Avoiding risk.** Risks – such as global tragedies, becoming ill, having an accident, making poor decisions or committing a social gaffe – are unavoidable and ever-present. You may be trying to eliminate risk by staying home or in 'safe' places eating only certain foods, never deviating from set routines, over-planning for trips away, or over-preparing for unlikely events such as war, plague or famine. In fact, risk is a part of life and can only be avoided to a limited extent. The more you try to eliminate all risk from your life, the more you're likely to focus on all the possible things that could go wrong. You're fighting a losing battle and are likely to undermine your sense of security even further. Focusing too much on the risks inherent in every day life will leave you chronically worried and cause you to overestimate the probability of bad things happening to you.

✔ **Trying to influence others.** Examples of influencing others' behaviour include encouraging your partner to socialise only with members of the same sex, persuading your children to stay at home rather than go out with their friends, and asking your doctor to send you for yet another test. Demanding that other people act in ways to minimise your intolerance of uncertainty and risk can seriously damage your relationships. People close to you are likely to perceive you as controlling or suspicious.

Try to understand that uncertainty has always been a major feature of the world, and that people still manage to keep themselves safe and secure. You don't need to change the world to feel secure. You simply need to accept uncertainty and live with it. You *can* happily coexist with uncertainty – it's always been that way. Remind yourself that ordinary people cope with bad events every day and that you're likely to cope as well as others do if something wicked your way comes.

The next section deals with accepting uncertainty and letting go of unhelpful coping strategies.

Surmounting the Side Effects of Excessive Safety-Seeking

One of the main ways in which you maintain emotional problems is by rescuing yourself from your imagined catastrophes. Often, these anticipated disasters are products of your worried mind, rather than real or probable events.

The actions that people take to prevent their feared catastrophes from occurring are called *safety behaviours*.

Avoiding, escaping or trying too hard to stop a feared catastrophe prevents you from realising three key things:

- ✔ Your feared event may never happen.
- ✔ If your feared event *does* happen, most likely you'll find ways to cope. For example, other people or organisations may be available to help you out.
- ✔ The feared event may well be inconvenient, uncomfortable, upsetting and deeply unpleasant, but rarely is it terrible or unbearable.

Anxiety affects your thinking in two key ways: it leads you to overestimate the probability and gravity of danger, and to underestimate your ability to overcome adversity. Of course you want to keep yourself as safe as possible. But sometimes you may try to keep yourself safe from events that really aren't that dangerous.

Additionally, some of the things that you do to eliminate risk and safeguard yourself may actually result in more discomfort and disturbance than necessary – using ultimately unhelpful strategies to avoid feared outcomes is very prevalent in anxiety disorders. Here are some examples of counterproductive safety behaviours that you might be using to cope with specific anxiety problems:

- ✔ **Panic attacks:** Michael's panic attacks are maintained by his fear that feeling dizzy will make him collapse. Whenever he feels dizzy, he takes a sip of water, sits down or holds on to something. In this way, he prevents himself from finding out that he won't collapse simply because he feels dizzy.

- ✔ **Social anxiety:** Sally tends to over-prepare what she's going to say before she actually says it. She monitors her speech and body language and reviews in her mind what she did and said when she gets home. In this way, she maintains her excessive self-consciousness.

- ✔ **Post-traumatic stress:** Since she had a car accident, Nina avoids motorways, grips tightly on to the steering wheel when driving in her car, repeatedly checks the rear-view mirror, and avoids being a car passenger. Because she's being so careful, her anxiety about having another accident remains at the forefront of her mind.

- ✔ **Agoraphobia:** Georgina's afraid of travelling far from her home or familiar places for fear of losing control of her bowels and soiling herself. She has become almost housebound, and she relies heavily on her husband to drive her around. This means that she doesn't go out on her own and never discovers that her fears are unfounded.

- ✔ **Fear of heights:** James is afraid of heights because he believes that the 'pulling' sensation he experiences in high places means that he's at risk of unintentionally throwing himself to his death. To cope with this sensation, he digs his heels firmly into the ground and leans slightly backwards to resist his feelings. He also tries to avoid high places as much as he can. These behaviours fuel his fear and leave him believing that somehow he's more at risk than other people in high places.

After you've drawn up a list of your avoidance and safety behaviours, you can have a better understanding of what areas you need to target for change. In essence, the real solution to your problem lies in exposing yourself to feared situations without using any safety behaviours. You can then see that you are able to cope with anxiety-provoking events and that you need not rely on distractions or spurious attempts to keep yourself safe. Give yourself the chance to see that your anxiety is not harmful in itself and that anxious feelings diminish if you let them do so of their own accord. (Chapter 8 contains more information about dealing with safety behaviours and devising exposures.)

Wending Your Way Out of Worry

One of the dilemmas faced by people who worry too much is how to reduce that worry. Some degree of worry is entirely normal – of course problems and responsibilities will cross your mind from time to time. Yet, you may be someone who worries all of the time. Being a true worrywart is intensely uncomfortable. Understandably, you may want to stop worrying quite so much.

Two reasons may account for your excessive worrying:

- ✔ You may think that by worrying about unpleasant events, you can prevent those events from happening. Or, you may believe that your worry can give you clues as to how to prevent negative events from coming to fruition.

- ✔ You may think that worry protects you by preparing you for negative events. You may believe that if you worry about bad things enough, they won't catch you off guard and you'll be better fixed to deal with them.

If you can convince yourself that excessive worry really doesn't prevent feared events from happening or prepare you for dealing with bad things, you may be in a better position to interrupt your repetitive cycle of worries.

Ironically, many people worry about things in a vain attempt to get all possible worries out of the way so they can then relax. Of course, this never happens – worry's a moveable feast, and something else always comes along for you to worry about.

If you worry excessively about everyday events, you may try to solve every possible upcoming problem in advance of it happening. You may hope that your worry will solve potential problems, and thus you won't have to worry about them any more.

Unfortunately, trying too hard to put your mind at rest can lead to increased mental activity and yet more worry. All too often, people then worry that worrying so much is harmful, and they end up worrying about worrying!

 Try to see your worrying as a bad habit. Instead of focusing on the content of your worries, try to interrupt the worry process by engaging your mind and body in activities outside of yourself.

Stopping Problems Perpetuating

Sometimes, the things you do to cope with your problems can bring about the very things that you're trying to avoid. An example of this is when you try to push upsetting thoughts out of your mind. Pushing away unpleasant thoughts is called *thought suppression*, and can generally make unwanted thoughts intrude more often. Research shows that when people try to suppress an unwanted thought, it can intrude into their mind twice as often than if they accept the thought and let it pass.

 Close your eyes and try really hard not to think of a pink elephant. Just for a minute, really push any images of pink elephants out of your mind. What happened? Most people notice that all they can think of are pink elephants. This demonstrates that trying to get rid of thoughts by pushing them out of your mind usually results in them hanging around more persistently.

Trying too hard not to do, feel or think specific things, and attempting to prevent certain events, can actually bring about what you most fear and wish to avoid. For example:

- ✔ Trying too hard not to make a fool of yourself in social situations can make you seem aloof and uninterested.

- ✔ Trying too hard to make sure a piece of work is perfect can lead you to miss a deadline, or become so nervous that you produce poor work.

✔ Insisting that you must succeed at a task, like passing an exam or learning a skill, makes you concentrate too much on *how well* you're doing and not enough on *what* you're doing.

✔ Feeling jealous and repeatedly checking up on your partner, testing them or demanding reassurance that they're not about to leave you, can potentially drive your partner away.

✔ Lying in bed, trying to deal with fatigue when you're depressed, can lower your mood further and may lead to feelings of shame and guilt about your inactivity.

Drop the shovel and empty your pockets!

One of the best metaphors for the kinds of behaviour we discuss in this chapter is the idea that some of your coping strategies may be like unwittingly trying to dig your way out of a hole. Naturally, the first step to overcoming your problems is to put down the shovel – to stop your self-defeating strategies, and gradually work out more productive ways of overcoming your emotional problems.

Over time, you may seek out bigger and better shovels in the guise of bigger and better avoidance and safety behaviours. We regularly invite those of our clients who suffer with agoraphobia, panic attacks, obsessive-compulsive disorder and body dysmorphic disorder, to share with us the contents of their pockets or handbags, which is often very illuminating. Examples of *safety props* that people carry 'just in case' include over-the-counter drugs, packets of tissues, antiseptic wipes, glucose sweets, handheld fans, make-up, plastic bags, paper bags, deodorant sprays, laxatives and alcohol.

To help clients eliminate safety behaviours, we often encourage them to throw out or hand over these seemingly innocent everyday items in the spirit of getting rid of problematic solutions. Go through your pockets and handbag and collect all of your safety props. Throw them in the bin or hand them over to someone who knows about your problems and has an interest in helping you (this person can be anyone in your life if you aren't currently seeing a CBT therapist). Be wary of purchasing or accumulating items to replace what you've already handed over or tossed away. Work on the basis that you only need essentials in your purse and pockets such as money, keys and travel cards.

Chapter 7

Setting Your Sights on Goals

• •

In This Chapter

▶ Defining your goals for emotional and behavioural change

▶ Motivating yourself

▶ Recording your progress

• •

*I*f we had to define the purpose of therapy, its purpose would *not* be to make you a straighter-thinking, more rational person. Rather, the purpose of therapy is to help you achieve your goals. Thinking differently is one way of achieving those goals. CBT can help you change the way you feel and behave. This chapter helps you define your goals and suggests some sources of inspiration for change.

Aaron Beck, founder of cognitive therapy, says that CBT is whatever helps you move from your problems to your goals. This definition emphasises the pragmatic and flexible nature of CBT, and encourages clients and therapists to select from a wide range of psychological techniques to help achieve goals in therapy. The crucial message, though, is that effective therapy is a constructive process, helping you to achieve your goals.

Putting SPORT into Your Goals

Many people struggle to overcome their problems because their goals are too vague. To help you develop goals that are clearer and easier to set your sights on, we developed the acronym SPORT, which stands for:

✔ **Specific:** Be precise about where, when and/or with whom you want to feel or behave differently. For example, you may want to feel concerned rather than anxious about making a presentation at work, and during the presentation you may want to concentrate on the audience rather than on yourself.

✔ **Positive:** State your goals in positive terms, encouraging yourself to develop more, rather than less, of something. For example, you may want to gain more confidence (rather than become less anxious) or to hone a skill (rather than make fewer mistakes).

Think of therapy as a journey. You're more likely to end up where you want to be if you focus on getting to your destination rather than on what you're trying to get away from.

✔ **Observable:** Try to include in your goal a description of a behavioural change that you can observe. Then, you can tell when you've achieved your goal because you can see a specific change.

If you're finding it hard to describe an observable change, think to yourself: 'How would the Martians, looking down from Mars, know I felt better simply by watching me?'

✔ **Realistic:** Make your goals clear, concrete, realistic and achievable. Focus on goals that are within your reach, and that depend on change from you rather than from other people. Try to visualise yourself achieving your goals. Realistic goals help you to stay motivated and focused.

✔ **Time:** Set a timeframe to keep you focused and efficient in your pursuit of a goal. For example, if you've been avoiding something for a while, decide when you plan to tackle it. Specify how long and how often you wish to carry out a new behaviour, such as going to the gym three times a week for an hour at a time.

Some goals, such as recovering from severe depression, can vary a lot in terms of how long they take to achieve. Setting schedules too rigidly can lead you to become depressed or angry at your lack of progress. So, set your deadlines firmly but flexibly, accept yourself if you don't achieve them on time, and persevere!

Homing In on How You Want to Be Different

Defining your goals and writing them down on paper forms the foundation of your CBT programme. This section helps you identify how you may want to feel and act differently.

Setting goals in relation to your current problems

To set a goal concerned with overcoming an emotional problem, you first need to define the problem, which we talk about in Chapter 56 (where we explore unhealthy emotions and behaviours and their healthy counterparts). Also refer to Chapter 6, in which we explore how attempts to make yourself feel better can sometimes make problems worse.

A *problem statement* contains the following components:

- ✔ Feelings/emotions

- ✔ A situation or theme that triggered your emotion

- ✔ The way you tend to act in the situation when you feel your problem emotion

Defining how you want to feel as an alternative

CBT can help you attain changes in the way you feel emotionally. For example, you may decide that you want to feel sad and disappointed, rather than depressed and hurt, about the end of your marriage.

Aiming to feel 'okay', 'fine' or 'relaxed' may not fit the bill if you're dealing with a tough situation. Feeling negative emotions about negative events is realistic and appropriate. Keep your goals realistic and helpful by aiming to have healthy emotions, and try to maintain an appropriate level of intensity of your emotions when faced with difficult events (take a look at Chapter 5 for more on healthy emotions).

Defining how you want to act

The second area of change that CBT can help you with is your behaviour. For example, after going through a divorce, you may decide that you want to begin seeing your friends and return to work, instead of staying in bed and watching TV all day.

You can also include changes to your mental activities within your goal, such as refocusing your attention on the outside world or allowing *catastrophic* (upsetting or worst-case scenario) thoughts to pass through your mind.

Making a statement

A *goal statement* is very similar to a problem statement – they have the same components, but the emotions and behaviours are different. A good goal statement involves the following:

To feel_____ (emotion) about_____ _____(theme or situation) and to_____ _____(behaviour).

So, for example, you may want to feel *concerned* (emotion) about *saying something foolish at a dinner party* (situation) and to *stay at the table in order to make further conversation* (behaviour).

Maximising Your Motivation

Motivation has a funny way of waxing and waning, just like the moon. Luckily, you don't necessarily have to feel motivated about changing before you can take steps forward. Motivation often follows rather than precedes positive action – often people find they 'get into' something once they've started.

Identifying inspiration for change

Lots of people find change difficult. Your motivation may flag sometimes, or you may not ever be able to imagine overcoming your difficulties. If either of these situations sounds familiar to you, you're in good company. Many people draw on sources of inspiration when starting with, and persevering through, the process of overcoming emotional problems. Sources of encouragement worth considering include the following:

✔ **Role models who have characteristics you aspire to adopt yourself.** For example, you may know someone who stays calm, expresses feelings to others, is open-minded to new experiences, or is assertive and determined. Whether real-life or fictional, alive or dead, known to you or someone you've never met, choose someone who inspires you and can give you a model for a new way of being.

✔ **Inspirational stories of people overcoming adversity.** Ordinary people regularly survive the most extraordinary experiences. Stories of their personal experiences can lead you to make powerful personal changes.

Focus on taking a leaf out of an inspirational individual's book, not on comparing yourself negatively with someone's 'superior' coping skills.

✔ **Images and metaphors.** Think of yourself as, for example, a sturdy tree withstanding a strong wind blowing against you, which can be an inspiring metaphor to represent you withstanding unreasonable criticism.

✔ **Proverbs, quotes and icons.** Use ideas you've heard expressed in novels, literature, films, songs or quotes to keep you reaching for your goals.

Focusing on the benefits of change

People often maintain apparently unhelpful patterns of behaviour (such as consistently arriving late for work) because they focus on the short-term benefit (in this case, avoiding the anxiety of being on a crowded bus or train) at the time of carrying out that behaviour. However, away from the immediate discomfort, these same people may focus on wishing they were free from the restrictions of their emotional problem (able to travel carefree on public transport).

Completing a cost–benefit analysis

Carrying out a *cost–benefit analysis* (CBA) to examine the pros and cons of something can help galvanise your commitment to change:

✔ **Behaviours:** How helpful is this action to you? Does it bring short-term or long-term benefits?

✔ **Emotions:** How helpful is this feeling? For example, does feeling guilty or angry really help you?

✔ **Thoughts, attitudes or beliefs:** Where does thinking this way get you? How does this belief help you?

✔ **Options for solving a practical problem:** How can this solution work out? Is this really the best possible answer to the problem?

When using a CBA form remember to evaluate the pros and cons:

✔ In the short term

✔ In the long term

✔ For yourself

✔ For other people

Try to write CBA statements in pairs, particularly when you're considering changing the way you feel, act or think. What are the *advantages* of feeling anxiety? And the *disadvantages*? Write down pairs of statements for what you feel, do or think *currently*, and for other, healthier alternatives. Tables 7-1 and 7-2 show a completed CBA form.

Table 7-1   Cost–Benefit Analysis: 'Costs and Benefits of Saying What Comes Into My Mind and Paying Attention to the Conversation'

Costs	Benefits
I may end up saying something stupid.	I won't have to think so much and I might be able to relax.
I may not come up with the best thing to say.	I can be more spontaneous.
I may end up running off at the mouth and people might not like me.	I'll be able to concentrate on what's being said and I won't seem so distracted.

Table 7-2 Second Cost–Benefit Analysis: 'Costs and Benefits of Preparing in My Head What I'm Going to Say Before Speaking'	
Costs	*Benefits*
I end up feeling very tired after going out.	I can make sure I don't say something foolish.
I can't relax into the conversation.	I may think of something funny or entertaining to say.
Sometimes I feel like the conversation moves on before I've had the chance to think of the right thing to say.	I can take more care not to offend people.

After you've done a CBA, review it with a critical eye on the 'benefits' of staying the same and the 'costs' of change. You may decide that these costs and benefits are not strictly accurate. The more you can boost your sense that change can benefit you, the more motivated you can feel in working towards your goals.

Write out a motivational flashcard that states the *benefits of change* and *costs of staying the same*, drawn from your cost–benefit analysis. You can then refer to this card to give yourself a motivational boost when you need it.

Mercurial desires

People often find that they want to change their goals on a whim or a fancy. For example, you may have a goal of being more productive and advancing your position at work. Then, after going to a Summer Solstice rave, you decide that really your goal is to be free and to travel the world, communing with the essence of life. What you choose as your definitive goal is up to you. But be wary of being influenced too easily by whatever's foremost in your mind. Constantly abandoning former goals and adopting new ones can be a mask for avoidance and procrastination. Use the SPORT acronym, as described at the start of this chapter, to assess the durability and functionality of each of your chosen goals.

A large aspect of achieving a goal, whether learning to play the guitar or building up a business, is about accepting temporary discomfort in order to bring long-term benefit.

Recording your progress

Keeping records of your progress can help you stay motivated. If your motivation flags, spur yourself on towards your goal by reviewing how far you've come. Use a problem-and-goal sheet like that in Figure 7-1, to specify your problem and rate its intensity. Then define your goal, and rate your progress towards achieving it . Do this at regular intervals, such as every one or two weeks.

1. **Identify the problem you're tackling.** Include information about the emotions and behaviours related to a specific event. Remember, you're feeling an *emotion* about a *situation*, leading you to *behave* in a certain way.

2. **At regular intervals, evaluate the intensity of your emotional problem and how much it interferes with your life.** 0 equals no emotional distress, and no interference in your life, and 10 equals maximum possible emotional distress, at great frequency, with great interference in your life.

3. **Fill in the goal section, keeping the theme or situation the same, but specifying how you wish to feel and act differently.**

4. **Rate how close you are to achieving your goal.** 0 equals no progress whatsoever, at any time, and 10 means that the change in your emotion and behaviour is completely and consistently achieved.

Using the form below, identify one of the main problems you wish to work on in therapy. A problem statement includes information about the emotions and behaviour related to a specific situation or event. For example: **'Feeling depressed about the end of my marriage leading me to become withdrawn and spend until around 6pm each day in bed'** or **'Feeling anxious about social situations leading me to avoid going to pubs, restaurants, and meetings, or to be extremely careful about what I say if I do socialise'**. Think of writing your problem statement as filling in blanks: **Feeling** _____ (emotion) about _____ (situation), leading me to _____ (behaviour).
Use the same format to identify the goal you would like to achieve, but this time specify how you would like things to be different in terms of your emotions and behaviour.

PROBLEM No. ☐	DATE:	DATE:	DATE:	DATE:	DATE:
	RATING:	RATING:	RATING:	RATING:	RATING:
	DATE:	DATE:	DATE:	DATE:	DATE:
	RATING:	RATING:	RATING:	RATING:	RATING:

Rate the severity of your emotional problem 0 - 10. **0 = No distress/No impairment in ability to function 10 = Extreme distress/Virtually unable to function in any area of life**

GOAL RELATED TO PROBLEM	DATE:	DATE:	DATE:	DATE:	DATE:
	RATING:	RATING:	RATING:	RATING:	RATING:
	DATE:	DATE:	DATE:	DATE:	DATE:
	RATING:	RATING:	RATING:	RATING:	RATING:

Rate how close you are to achieving your goal. **0 = No progress whatsoever 10 = Goal achieved and sustained consistently**

Figure 7-1: The Problem-and-Goal Sheet.

Part III

Putting CBT into Action

The 5th Wave   By Rich Tennant

"I sense that you're becoming more defensive and unapproachable lately."

In this part . . .

Sometimes it can seem as if no one understands your problem, but we do! These chapters give you CBT ammunition to surmount your problems and really begin to realise recovery.

Chapter 8

Standing Up to Anxiety and Facing Fear

nxiety is a bully. And like most bullies, the more you let it shove you around, the pushier it gets. This chapter helps you get to know the nature of anxiety and to identify the ways in which it pushes you about. Fundamentally, you can beat anxiety, like any bully, by standing up to it.

Acquiring Anti-Anxiety Attitudes

Your thoughts are what count, because your feelings are influenced greatly by how you think. Feeling anxious increases the chance of you experiencing anxiety-provoking thoughts (refer to Chapter 5). Anxious thoughts can increase anxious feelings, and so a vicious cycle can develop. You can help yourself to face your fears by adopting the attitudes we outline in this section.

Thinking realistically about the probability of bad events

If you have any kind of anxiety problem, you probably spend a lot of time worrying about bad things that *may* happen to you or your loved ones. The more you focus your attention on

negative events and worry about bad things being just around
the corner, the more likely you are going to believe that they'll
actually happen.

Proving for sure that bad events won't happen isn't that easy
without a crystal ball or two, but you can acknowledge that
you tend to *overestimate* the probability of bad things happening. Adjust your thinking appropriately to *counterbalance*
for this tendency. Counterbalancing your attitude is a lot like
riding a bike with the handlebars offset to the left – to steer
straight, you need to turn the handlebars to the right, otherwise you keep veering off to the left. If you tend to always
imagine the worst, straighten out your thinking by deliberately assuming that things are going to be okay.

Avoiding extreme thinking

Telling yourself that things are 'awful', 'horrible', 'terrible'
or 'the end of the world' only turns up the anxiety heat.
Remind yourself that few things are really that dreadful, and
instead rate events more accurately as 'bad', 'unfortunate' or
'unpleasant but not 'the end of the world'.

Extreme thinking leads to extreme emotional reactions. When
you mislabel a negative event as 'horrible', you make yourself
overly anxious about unpleasant but relatively non-extreme
events, such as minor public embarrassment.

Taking the fear out of fear

When people say things like 'Don't worry, it's *just* anxiety', the
word 'just' implies – wrongly – that anxiety's a mild experience. Anxiety can, in fact, be a very profound experience, with
strong bodily and mental sensations. Some anxious people
misinterpret these intense physical symptoms as dangerous
or as signs of impending peril. Common misreadings include
assuming that a nauseous feeling means that you're about to
be sick, or thinking that you're going crazy because your sur-
roundings feel 'unreal'.

If you have concerns about your physical sensations you may
consider seeing your family doctor prior to deliberately confronting your fears. Your doctor may then be able to advise
you as to whether deliberately increasing your anxiety in the

short term, in order to be free of it in the long term, is safe enough for you. It is rare for people to be advised against facing their fears.

Understanding and accepting common sensations of anxiety can help you stop adding to your anxiety by misinterpreting normal sensations as dangerous. Figure 8-1 outlines some of the more common physical aspects of anxiety.

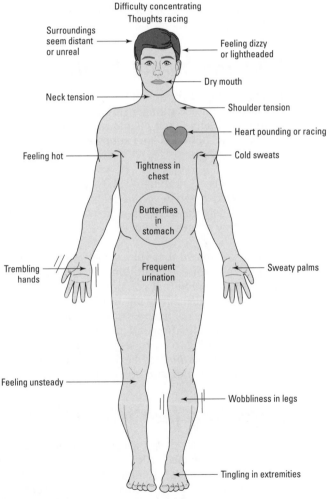

Figure 9-1: Common physical sensations of anxiety.

Undoubtedly, anxiety is an unpleasant, sometimes extremely disturbing experience. However, evaluating your anxiety as 'unbearable' or saying 'I can't stand it' only turns up the emotional heat. Remind yourself that anxiety is hard to bear but not unbearable.

Attacking Anxiety

The following are some key principles for targeting and destroying anxiety.

Winning by not fighting

Trying to control your anxiety can lead you to feeling more intensely anxious for longer (for more on this, read through Chapter 6). Many of our clients say to us: 'Facing my fears makes sense, but what am I supposed to do while I'm feeling anxious?'

The answer is . . . nothing. Well, sort of. Accepting and tolerating your anxiety when you're deliberately confronting your fears is usually the most effective way of making sure that your anxiety passes quickly.

 If you're convinced that your anxiety won't diminish by itself, even when you do nothing, test it out. Pick one anxiety-provoking situation that you normally withdraw from – examples include using a lift, travelling on a busy bus, standing in a crowded room and drinking alone in a bar. Make yourself stay in the situation and just let your anxiety do its thing. Don't do anything to try to stop the anxiety. Just stay where you are and *do nothing* other than feel anxious. Eventually, your anxiety will begin to ebb away.

Defeating fear with FEAR

Perhaps the most reliable way of overcoming anxiety is the following maxim: FEAR – Face Everything And Recover. Supported by numerous clinical trials, and used daily all over the world, the principle of facing your fears until your anxiety reduces is one of the cornerstones of CBT.

The process of deliberately confronting your fear and staying within the feared situation until your anxiety subsides is known as *exposure* or *desensitisation*. The process of getting used to something, like cold water in a swimming pool, is called *habituation*. The principle is to wait until your anxiety reduces by at least half before ending your session of exposure – usually between twenty minutes and one hour, but sometimes more.

Repeatedly confronting your fears

As Figure 8-2 shows, if you deliberately confront your fears, your anxiety becomes less severe and reduces more quickly with each exposure. The more exposures you experience, the better. When you first confront your fears, aim to repeat your exposures at least daily.

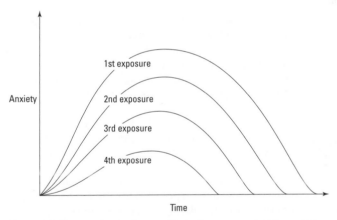

Figure 8-2: Your anxiety reduces with each exposure to a feared trigger.

Keeping your exposure challenging but not overwhelming

When confronting your fears, aim for *manageable exposure*, so that you can successfully experience facing your fears and mastering them. If your exposures are overwhelming, you may end up resorting to escape, avoidance or safety behaviours. The flipside of choosing overwhelming exposures is taking things too gently, which can make your progress slow and demoralising. Strive to strike a balance between the two extremes.

If you set yourself only easy, gentle exposures, you risk reinforcing the erroneous idea that anxiety is unbearable and must be avoided. The point of exposure work is to prove to yourself that you *can* bear the discomfort associated with anxious feelings.

Taking it step by step

Avoid overwhelming or underchallenging yourself by using a *graded hierarchy* of feared or avoided situations. A graded hierarchy is a way of listing your fears from the mildest to the most severe.

If you want to kill your fear, let it die of its own accord.

You can use the following table to list people, places, situations, objects, animals, sensations or whatever triggers your fear. Be sure to include situations that you tend to avoid. Rank these triggers in rough order of difficulty. Alongside each trigger, rate your anticipated level of anxiety on the good old 0–10 scale. *Voila!* You have a graded hierarchy.

After you have confronted your fear, rate the *actual* level of anxiety or discomfort you experienced. Then, tailor your next exposure session accordingly. Most situations are not as bad as you expect them to be. In the unlikely event that the reality is worse than your expectations, you may need to devise more manageable exposures for the next few steps and work your way up the hierarchy more gradually.

Table 8-1	Graded Hierarchy of Anxiety	
Feared or Avoided Trigger	*Anticipated Anxiety or Discomfort 0–10*	*Actual Anxiety or Discomfort 0–10*

Jumping in at the deep end

Although we caution about striking a balance between under- and overchallenging yourself, jumping in with both feet does have its benefits. The sooner you can face your biggest fears, the sooner you can master them. Consider whether you can climb to the top of your hierarchy straight away.

Graded exposure is a means to an end. Going straight to your worst-feared situation without resorting to safety behaviours (which we talk about in the next section) can help you get rapid results, as long as you stick with the exposure long enough to discover that nothing terrible happens.

Shedding safety behaviours

You can overcome anxiety by turning your anxiety upside-down. The best way to make your anxiety go away is to invite it to do its own thing. As we explain in a bit more detail in Chapter 6, the things you do to reduce your fear in the short term are often the very things that start you feeling anxious in the first place. (Check out Chapter 6 for some common examples of safety behaviours.)

Recording your fear-fighting

Keep a record of your work against fear so you can check out your progress and make further plans. Your record can include:

- ✔ The length of your exposure session
- ✔ Ratings of your anxiety at the beginning, middle and end of your exposure session.

A record helps you see whether you're sticking with your programme long enough for your fear to subside. If your fear doesn't seem to be reducing, make sure that you're still trying hard enough to reduce your fear by getting rid of those safety behaviours.

You can use the behavioural experiment record sheet in Chapter 4 to record your exposure and to compare your predicted outcome of confronting your fears with the actual outcome.

Overriding Common Anxieties

The following sections outline the application of CBT for some common anxiety problems. A full discussion of all of the specific types of anxiety problems lies outside the scope of this book. However, the CBT principles that we introduce you to here are the very best bet for overcoming most anxiety problems.

First, define what you're doing to keep your anxiety alive in your thinking (see Chapters 2 and 5), and alive in your behaviour (see Chapters 5 and 6). Then, start to catch your unhelpful thoughts and generate alternatives (Chapter 3), and test them out in reality (Chapter 4). Understanding where you focus your attention, and re-training your attention, can also be hugely helpful.

Socking it to social anxiety

Attack *social anxiety* (excessive fear of negative evaluation by other people) by drawing up a list of your feared and avoided social situations and the safety behaviours you tend to carry out (check out Chapter 6 for more on safety behaviours).

Hang on to the idea that you can accept yourself even if other people don't like you. Be more flexible about how witty, novel and entertaining you 'have' to be. Systematically test out your predictions about people thinking negatively about you – how do people act when you don't try so hard to perform? Refocus your attention on the world around you and the people you interact with, rather than on yourself. Once you've left the social situation, resist the tendency to play your social encounters back in your mind.

Waging war on worry

To wage war on your excessive worry, resist the temptation to try to solve every problem in advance of it happening. Try to live with doubt and realise that the most important thing is not what you specifically worry about but *how* you manage your worrying thoughts. Overcoming worry is the art of allowing thoughts to enter your mind without trying to 'sort them out' or push them away.

Pounding on panic

Panic attacks are intense bursts of anxiety in the absence of real danger, and can often seem to come out of the blue. Panic attacks often have very strong physical sensations such as nausea, heart palpitations, a feeling of shortness of breath, choking, dizziness and hot sweats. Panic sets in when people mistake these physical sensations as dangerous and get into a vicious cycle because these misinterpretations lead to more anxiety, leading to more physical sensations.

Put panic out of your life by deliberately triggering off panic sensations. Enter situations you've been avoiding and resist using safety behaviours. Realise, for example, that feeling dizzy doesn't cause you to collapse, so you don't need to sit down, and that other uncomfortable sensations of anxiety will pass without harming you. Carry out a behavioural experiment (see Chapter 4) to specifically test out whether your own feared catastrophes come true as a consequence of a panic attack.

Assaulting agoraphobia

Georgina was afraid to travel far from her home or from familiar places she felt safe in, which are common characteristics of *agoraphobia*. She feared losing control of her bowels and soiling herself. She had become virtually housebound and relied heavily on her husband to drive her around. She learned about the nature of anxiety and developed the theory that, although she may *feel* like she is going to soil herself, her sensations are due largely to anxiety and she will be able to 'hold on'.

To gain confidence and overcome agoraphobia, develop a hierarchy of your avoided situations and begin to face them, and stay in them until your anxiety reduces. This may include driving progressively longer distances alone, using public transport and walking around in unfamiliar places. At the same time, work hard to drop your safety behaviours so you can discover that nothing terrible happens if you do become anxious or panicky, and ride it out.

Dealing with post-traumatic stress disorder

Post-traumatic stress disorder (PTSD) can develop after being involved in (or witnessing) an accident, assault or other extremely threatening or distressing event. The symptoms of PTSD include being easily startled, feeling irritable and anxious, memories of the event intruding into your waking day, nightmares about the event or feeling emotionally numb. If you have PTSD you may be sustaining your distress by misunderstanding your normal feelings of distress in response to the event, trying to avoid triggers that activate memories of the event or trying too hard to keep yourself safe.

To combat PTSD, remind yourself that memories of a traumatic event intruding into your mind, and feelings of distress are normal reactions to trauma. Allowing memories to enter your mind and spending time thinking about them is part of processing traumatic events, and a crucial part of recovery. Many people find that deliberately confronting triggers or writing out a detailed first-person account can be helpful. At the same time it's important to reduce any excessive safety precautions you may have begun to take.

Hitting back at fear of heights

Begin to attack a fear of heights by carrying out a survey among your friends about the kind of feelings that they have when standing at the edge of a cliff or at the top of a tall building (see Chapter 4 for more on conducting surveys). You'll probably discover that your sensation of being unwillingly drawn over the edge is very common. Most people, however, just interpret this feeling as a normal reaction.

Put this new understanding into action to gain more confidence about being in high places. Work through a hierarchy of entering increasingly tall buildings, looking over bridges and climbing to the top of high cliffs.

Fascinating phobias

One of the interesting things about anxiety problems is the wide variety of things that human beings fear. In our practice, we still encounter people with fears we've never heard of before. Crucially, what matters is not what you're afraid of but how negatively your fear is affecting your life.

Sometimes people are embarrassed by their phobias because they think others may find them silly or trivial. But extreme fear is never trivial – terror and fear can be very disabling, even if your fear is of something as simple as buttons. We suggest you seek out health professionals who take you seriously so you can get help for your phobia.

Common phobias include:

- ✓ **Acrophobia:** fear of heights or high levels

- ✓ **Agoraphobia:** fear of open spaces, crowded public places or being away from a place of safety

- ✓ **Aichmophobia:** fear of pins, needles and pointed objects

- ✓ **Arachnophobia:** fear of spiders

- ✓ **Claustrophobia:** fear of confined or small spaces

- ✓ **Emetophobia:** fear of vomiting

- ✓ **Haemophobia:** fear of blood and blood injury

- ✓ **Lockiophobia:** fear of childbirth

- ✓ **Noctiphobia:** fear of the night and the dark

- ✓ **Trypanophobia:** fear of injections

Less common phobias include:

- ✓ **Arachibutyrophobia**: fear of peanut butter sticking to the roof of one's mouth

- ✓ **Automatonophobia**: fear of ventriloquists' dummies, dolls, animatronic creatures or wax statues

- ✓ **Barophobia:** fear of gravity

- ✓ **Bibliophobia:** fear of books (if you've got this one, stick with us – you're doing well!)

- ✓ **Blennophobia:** fear of slime

- ✓ **Lutraphobia:** fear of otters

- ✓ **Lyssophobia:** fear of going insane

- ✓ **Necrophobia:** fear of death or dead things

- ✓ **Ombrophobia:** fear of rain or being rained on

- ✓ **Soceraphobia:** fear of parents-in-law

Chapter 9

Deconstructing and Demolishing Depression

· ·

In This Chapter

▶ Understanding depression

▶ Identifying thinking and behaviour patterns that keep your depression going

▶ Recognising and reducing ruminative thinking

▶ Confronting and solving practical problems

▶ Using activity as an antidepressant

▶ Getting your sleeping pattern back on track

· ·

*S*tatistics show that as many as one in two people are estimated to experience depression at some point in their lives. Luckily, the problem is well-recognised and treatable.

If, for the past month, you've felt down, lacked energy, been pessimistic or hopeless about the future, and lost interest or enjoyment in doing things, then you may be suffering from depression. If you've also had difficulty concentrating, had a poor appetite, been waking early, and experienced a low mood, anxious thoughts or feelings of dread in the morning, then you're even more likely to be depressed. If you have three or more of these symptoms, your symptoms have been present for two weeks or more, and are intense enough to interrupt your usual day-to-day activities, then we recommend that you visit your doctor and investigate the possibility that you're suffering from depression.

Antidepressant medication can help to alleviate some of your depressive symptoms, although not every person diagnosed with depression needs to take medication. Depending on the severity of your depression, a course of CBT treatment may be enough to help you get better.

Looking at what Fuels Depression

Unfortunately, certain things that you do, in an attempt to alleviate your feelings of depression, may actually be making your symptoms worse. When people are depressed, they often make the mistake of doing what their mood dictates.

CBT helps depressed individuals learn to override their depressed mood and to do the *opposite* of what their depression makes them *feel like doing*. Here are some of the main actions and thoughts that actually stoke depression:

- ✔ **Rumination:** Getting hooked into a repetitive, cyclical process of negative thinking, repeatedly going over problems in the past or asking yourself unanswerable questions.

- ✔ **Negative thinking:** In depression, your negative thoughts about yourself are often based on beliefs that you're helpless and worthless. Thoughts about the world being an unsafe and undesirable place to live in are also a common feature of depression.

- ✔ **Inactivity:** Feeling that you can't be bothered to do day-to-day tasks, not participating in activities that previously you enjoyed and staying in bed because you don't believe you can face the day.

- ✔ **Social withdrawal:** Avoiding seeing other people and not interacting with the people around you.

- ✔ **Procrastination:** Avoiding specific tasks, such as paying bills, booking appointments and making phone calls, because you think they're too difficult or scary to confront.

- ✔ **Shame:** Feeling ashamed about your depression, and telling yourself that other people would judge you harshly if they knew how much your effectiveness and productivity had decreased.

> ✔ **Guilt:** Feeling guilty about your depression, and overestimating the degree to which your low mood causes inconvenience and suffering for your loved ones.
>
> ✔ **Hopelessness:** Thinking that you'll never feel better or that your situation will never improve.

Depression typically dulls your ability to glean enjoyment from previously enjoyed activities. Be patient with yourself and trust that your feelings of enjoyment can return over time. In the first instance, it's enough to simply do the things that you've been avoiding *for the sake of it.* Doing something is better than doing nothing. Don't put pressure on yourself to 'have a good time' at this early stage in your recovery.

Going Round and Round in Your Head: Ruminative Thinking

Rumination is an integral process in maintaining your depression. Most people with depression are likely to engage in some rumination, even if they're not aware that they do.

Rumination is a circular thought process in which you go over the same things again and again. Often, the focus is on how bad you feel or doubting that you can ever feel differently or better. Your rumination may also focus on trying to work out the root cause of your depression, or on the events that have contributed to you being depressed. You may ask yourself questions like the following, over and over again:

> ✔ Why is this happening to me?
>
> ✔ What could I have done to stop this happening?
>
> ✔ If only *x*, *y* or *z* hadn't happened, I'd be okay.

Depression makes people feel compelled to ruminate. In a sense, rumination is like a faulty attempt to solve problems. Rumination is compelling because your depressed mood tells you that you must try to get to the bottom of why you feel bad. But rumination simply doesn't work: you end up trying to solve your depression by going over the same old ground and looking for answers inside the problem. You focus your attention on how depressed you feel, which leads to you feeling more depressed.

Fortunately, you can catch yourself going into a ruminative state by using the techniques we discuss in the following sections to interrupt the process.

Catching yourself in the act

Rumination is all-consuming. It will typically absorb you quite totally. You may look like you're simply staring blankly into space, but in your head your thoughts are going ten to the dozen. The key is to know when you're going *into* rumination, so you can take steps towards *getting out* of rumination.

Early warning signs of rumination taking hold include the following:

- ✔ **Getting stuck.** You may be in the middle of doing something and find that you've stopped moving and are deep in thought. For example, you may be perching on the side of the bed for several minutes (or even much longer!) when actually you intended going for a shower.

- ✔ **Feeling low.** Beware of times when your mood's at its lowest ebb: this is when you're most likely to engage in rumination. Most people ruminate at particular times of the day, more often than other times (although rumination can happen at any time).

- ✔ **Slowing down.** You may be doing something and then start to move more slowly, like pausing in the aisle at the supermarket. You start to slow down because your concentration's heading elsewhere.

- ✔ **Getting repetitive.** The same old thoughts and questions drift into your head, time and time again. You get a familiar niggling feeling that these vague questions must be answered.

The content of your ruminations isn't the problem – the process of rumination itself is.

Arresting ruminations before they arrest you

Several different tricks can help you stop the rumination process. Try some of the following:

- ✔ **Get busy.** Perhaps one of the most effective strategies you can adopt is to make your body and mind busy with something outside yourself. If you're vitally absorbed in an activity, you may find it harder to engage in rumination. These types of activity may include doing the housework with the radio on to hold your attention away from your internal thoughts, making a phone call, surfing the Internet, running errands, taking the dogs for a walk, and so on.

- ✔ **Work out.** Hard aerobic exercise can exorcise those toxic thought processes. Be sure to exercise during the day or in the early morning, because exercising too near bedtime can disturb your sleep.

- ✔ **Get up and out.** Rumination's more difficult when you're outside of your home or in the company of others. If you know that you're most vulnerable to ruminating at certain hours of the day, make sure that you schedule activities for these times.

- ✔ **Let your thoughts go.** Practise letting your negative thoughts pass by and simply observe them like pictures across a television screen. Don't engage with your negative thoughts, judge them or try to answer any questions – just accept their existence and let them slip by.

- ✔ **Get good at redirecting your attention.** You can strengthen your attention muscles and deliberately focus on less depressing things. Try using *task concentration* *training*, a method of attending to external aspects of your environment, as it can successfully interrupt rumination.

✔ **Be sceptical.** Your depressed thoughts are a symptom of your depression, so try to take them with a sizable pinch of salt. You can resist the urge to ruminate about your depressed thoughts by deciding that they're neither true nor important. Even though they *feel* important and worthy of scrutiny – they aren't. You won't learn anything new about your depression by focusing on negative repetitive thoughts.

Keeping busy is a great technique for interrupting ruminative thinking. However, you can still end up ruminating while you're engaged in an activity. Be aware of paying attention to whatever you're doing.

Activating Yourself as an Antidepressant

Withdrawal and inactivity are the two most fundamental *maintaining factors* in depression – they keep you in a vicious cycle of isolation and low mood. For example, to counteract feelings of fatigue, you may be tempted (very tempted) to spend more time in bed. Unfortunately, remaining in bed means more inactivity and less energy.

If you feel ashamed of being 'flat', about having nothing to say, or feel guilty about burdening your friends, then keeping to yourself may seem sensible. The problem is that the less you do and the fewer people you see, the less pleasure and satisfaction you'll get out of life, the less support you'll receive, and the more your problems will pile up and weigh heavy on your mind. Staying away from others may *seem* like the right thing to do when your mood is low. You may believe that you've got nothing to offer others. You may even have thoughts about being undeserving of friendship or love. However, the more you act on these destructive ideas, the more you reinforce them and convince yourself that they're true. Following your depressive tendency to isolate yourself can lead into true loneliness.

You don't necessarily have to talk about your low feelings when you see friends; in fact, it's often a good idea not to. Talking about superficial things and listening to what others have been up to can give you a welcome break from your own thoughts. Try not to worry about making interesting conversation and just allow yourself to absorb the company of those you're with.

Because depressive illness trains you to be such a skilled self-saboteur, you may end up doing negative self-comparisons when in company. Be wary of letting stealthy depressed thoughts such as 'I should be getting on with my life like my friends are' or 'Why can't I be happy like so and so?' take hold.

Tackling inactivity

One of the best ways of starting to overcome depression is to gradually become more active, to steadily re-engage with other people, and to start tackling daily chores and other problems.

Use the activity schedule in Table 9-1 to start to plan each day with a realistic balance of activities and rest. Build up your activities gradually. If you've been in bed for days, getting out of the bedroom and sitting in a chair is a big move in the right direction. Remember: take it step by step. Using the activity schedule is really simple; it merely involves allocating a specific time to do a specific activity. You can photocopy the blank schedule in Table 9-1 and fill it in.

Don't overload your activity schedule, otherwise you may feel overwhelmed, sink back into inactivity, and probably berate yourself for being ineffective. It's crucial to *realistically* plan a gradual increase in activities, starting from where you are *now*, not from where you think you *should* be.

Table 9-1   **Activity Schedule**

	Monday	Tuesday	Wednesday	Thursday	Friday	Saturday	Sunday
6–8 a.m.							
8–10							
10–12							
12–2 p.m.							
2–4							
4–6							
6–8							
8–10							

Dealing with the here and now: Solving problems

As with other aspects of your daily or weekly activities, you need to be steady and systematic in your attempts to deal with practical problems, such as paying bills, writing letters, and completing other tasks that can pile up when you're less active.

To get started, set aside a specific amount of time each day for dealing with neglected chores. Allocating your time can help things seem more manageable. Try the following problem-solving process:

1. **Define your problem.**

   At the top of a sheet of paper, write down the problems you're struggling with. For example, you might consider problems with the following:

   - Relationships
   - Isolation
   - Interests and hobbies
   - Employment and education
   - Financial issues
   - Legal issues
   - Housing
   - Health

Apply the following steps to each of your identified problems. You may need to do Steps 2 to 5 on each of your different problems.

2. **Brainstorm solutions to your problem.**

   Write down all the possible solutions you can think of. Consider the following questions to help you generate some solutions:

   - How did you deal with similar problems in the past?

- How have other people coped with similar problems?

- How do you imagine you'd tackle the problem if you weren't feeling depressed?

- How do you think someone else would approach the problem?

- What resources (such as professionals and voluntary services) can you access for help with your problems?

3. **Evaluate your solutions.**

    Review your 'brainstormed' list. Select some of your most realistic seeming solutions, and list the pros and cons of each.

4. **Try out a solution.**

    On the basis of your evaluation of pros and cons, choose a solution to try out.

You can easily feel overwhelmed when your mood is low. Even the best of solutions can seem too difficult. To deal with this, break down your solution into a series of smaller, more manageable steps.

5. **Review.**

    After trying out a solution, review how much it has helped you to resolve your problem. Consider whether you need to take further steps, try another solution or move on to tackling another problem.

Taking care of yourself and your environment

One of the hallmarks of depression is neglecting yourself and your living environment, which in turn leaves you feeling more depressed.

Include bathing, laundry, tidying and cleaning as part of your weekly activity schedule.

Getting a Good Night's Sleep

Sleep disturbance, in one form or another, can often accompany depression. Here are some tips you can use to improve your chances of greeting the sandman:

- ✔ **Get some exercise.** We cannot overstate the benefits of taking regular exercise. Exercise is good for your mood and good for your sleeping. You can take vigorous exercise during the day or even first thing in the morning to get your *endorphins* ('feel good' chemicals in your brain) charging. If you want to take some exercise in the evenings to help you wind down and de-stress, keep it gentle and not too close to your bedtime. A stroll, or an easy cycle ride, is an ideal choice.

- ✔ **Establish a schedule.** Getting up at the same time every day and avoiding daytime naps can help you get your sleeping back on track. Catnapping may be very tempting, but ultimately it interferes with your bedtime and can actually lower your mood. If you know that you get the urge for a siesta around the same time every day, make plans to be out of the house at this time. Make yourself busy to keep yourself awake.

- ✔ **Avoid lying in bed awake.** If you find dropping off to sleep difficult, don't lie in bed tossing and turning. Get out of bed and do something – ideally, something like sorting laundry or reading a book until you feel ready for sleep. Try to stay up until your eyelids start to feel heavy. The same applies if you wake in the middle of the night and can't get back to sleep easily. Don't stay in bed for longer than ten minutes trying to get back to sleep. Get up and do something like the above ideas, then get back into bed only when you feel sleepy.

- ✔ **Watch your caffeine and stimulant intake.** Avoid caffeinated drinks from mid- to late afternoon.

- ✔ **Establish a bedtime routine.** Going through the same pre-bedtime procedures each night can help your mind realise that it's getting near to shutdown time.

Setting realistic sleep expectations

During the day and while you try to fall asleep, you may well have thoughts like 'I'll never be able to get to sleep', or 'I'm in for another night of waking up every two hours'. Understandably, you may have these expectations if your sleep has been disturbed for some time, but such thinking is likely to perpetuate your sleep disturbance. Be aware of your worrying thoughts about sleep problems, such as 'I'll never be able to cope on such little sleep', or 'I've got to get some sleep tonight'. Trying to force yourself to go to sleep is rarely successful, and doing so contradicts the concept of *relaxation* because you're making an *effort* to sleep.

Considering compassion

You can't bully yourself out of depression. If that strategy worked, we'd have far fewer clients. Giving yourself a hard time for being low is literally kicking yourself when you're down. So many depressed people both berate and refuse to look after themselves because doing so's part of an insidious cycle. See Figure 9-1.

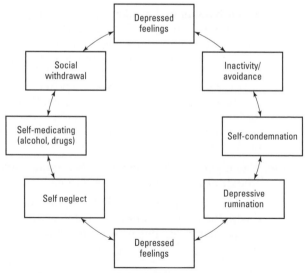

Figure 9-1: The cycle of depression.

When you're ill, you want to get well again. That involves looking after yourself, both mentally and physically. When you have flu or some other physical illness, you probably don't tell yourself that you should never have become ill in the first place, or that you're weak and pathetic because you've done so. Depression is a different ball game, as Figure 9-1 illustrates. An essential part of recovery is offering yourself compassion instead of criticism. Try these tips for being kind to yourself:

- ✔ **Give yourself credit for your efforts to act against depression.** Instead of telling yourself that you should be doing more, start from where you are now. If yesterday you didn't get out of bed and today you did – that's significant progress. The next step may be going to the shops or answering your telephone. Focus on your small daily improvements instead of benchmarking yourself against where you ultimately want to be.

- ✔ **Compliment and kindly cajole yourself.** Depression inevitably invites you to think of yourself in negative ways and call yourself bad names. Stop yourself from verbalising or mentally constructing self-directed insults. Instead, deliberately call to mind your good points and encourage yourself to do more through the use of praise. Be nice!

- ✔ **Be wary of false friends.** Using illicit drugs, alcohol or food to alleviate your feelings and thoughts can grant you a brief respite – but at a high cost. You're likely to feel far worse when you 'come down' from drugs and alcohol or after an eating binge. You may end up with a dependency that prolongs a period of depression which may otherwise shortly relent. Alcohol and drug use can also interfere with the effectiveness of antidepressant medication.

Obtaining a new outlook

A depressed outlook is typically bleak. The future seems impossible to contemplate because everything seems tinged with grey. Constructing a new optimistic outlook and practising it daily – even several times each day – can be useful. You may not feel as though you believe it at first but, with time, this bright outlook will probably begin to ring true. Try adopting these new outlooks:

- ✔ 'I look forward to feeling better soon.'

- ✔ 'I may not see the light at the end of the tunnel but I know it's there.'

    ✔ 'This will pass.'

    ✔ 'I'll deal with the future when it comes; I don't need to worry about it now.'

    ✔ 'Hanging on is worth it because things will get better.'

The road to recovery from depression is rarely a steady uphill climb. Setbacks and difficult days are part and parcel of a normal recovery. Don't be too disappointed if, after a series of good days, you have a hard one. This difficult day isn't a return to square one or a sign that you're not improving.

Managing Suicidal Thoughts

The most dangerous element of depression is that the feelings of hopelessness you can experience may become so strong that you try to take your own life. Don't panic about having suicidal thoughts if you're depressed. Such thoughts are very common and having them doesn't necessarily mean that you'll act on them.

If you've been feeling very hopeless about the future and have started to make plans about how to kill yourself, *you must immediately seek medical assistance.* Go to see your regular doctor as a first point of call, or attend Accident and Emergency (Casualty) if you feel at risk of suicide outside of surgery hours.

Here are some tips on managing suicidal thoughts:

    ✔ Recognise your feelings of hopelessness about the future as a *symptom* of depression, not a fact.

    ✔ Remember that depression is a temporary state and there's lots of ways to treat it. Decide to tackle your depression for, say, six weeks, as an experiment to see whether things can improve.

    ✔ Tell a friend or family member how you're feeling.

    ✔ See a doctor and/or therapist, or join a support group for further help and support if you're finding it difficult to overcome your depression alone.

    ✔ Try instigating the problem-solving process we outline in the previous section in this chapter, for any problem you currently see as hopeless.

Famous and depressed

One of the most crucial aspects of recovering from depression is shedding any feelings of shame you may have about the problem. Realising that *no one* has a guarantee that they won't get depressed can help here. Depression has affected all kinds of people, from all walks of life, and of all creeds, colours and levels of intelligence.

Dozens of famous people have publicly reported or discussed their battles with depression during their lives. Celebrities are now 'coming out' about their suffering from depression or bipolar affective disorder (formerly known as manic depression). We hope that their actions can help to remove the stigma of mental health problems and enable more people to identify and seek help for depression.

Here are just a few famous types who've suffered from depression or bipolar affective disorder:

- Buzz Aldrin (astronaut)
- Ludwig van Beethoven (composer)
- William Blake (poet)
- Winston Churchill (British Prime Minister)
- John Cleese (comedian, actor and writer)
- Charles Dickens (writer)
- Germaine Greer (writer and journalist)
- Spike Milligan (comedian, actor and writer)
- Isaac Newton (physicist)
- Mary Shelley (writer)
- Vincent Van Gogh (artist)
- Lewis Wolpert (embryologist and broadcaster)

In our clinical practice we often treat doctors, psychiatrists and other mental health professionals for depression. So it just goes to show that anyone can suffer from psychological illness – even those who earn a living treating it.

Chapter 10

Overcoming Low Self-Esteem and Accepting Yourself

*D*isturbing feelings, such as depression, anxiety, shame, guilt, anger, envy and jealousy, are often rooted in low self-opinion. If you're prone to experiencing these feelings, then you may well have a problem with your self-esteem. You may assume that you're only as worthwhile as your achievements, love life, social status, attractiveness or financial prowess. If you link your worth to these *temporary conditions* and for some reason they diminish, your self-esteem can plummet too. Alternatively, you may take a long-standing dim view of yourself: However favourable the conditions mentioned above, your self-esteem may be chronically low. Whatever the case, you can follow the philosophy of self-acceptance that we outline in this chapter, which can significantly improve the attitude you hold towards yourself.

Identifying Issues of Self-Esteem

Implicit in the concept of self-esteem is the notion of *estimating*, or rating and measuring, your worth. If you have high self-esteem, then your measure of your value or worth is high. Conversely, if you have low self-esteem, your estimate of your value is low.

Condemning yourself globally is a form of overgeneralising, known as *labelling* or *self-downing*. This thinking error creates low self-esteem. Labelling yourself makes you feel worse and can lead to counterproductive actions, such as avoidance, isolation, rituals, procrastination and perfectionism:

I'm disgusting	I'm a failure	I'm stupid
I'm inferior	I'm useless	I'm less worthwhile
I'm inadequate	I'm not good enough	I'm bad
I'm unlovable	I'm worthless	I'm defective
I'm incompetent	I don't matter	I'm pathetic
I'm weak	I'm no good	I'm a loser

Developing Self-Acceptance

One approach to tackling your low self-esteem is to boost the estimate you have of your worth. The underlying problem, however, still remains. Self-acceptance is an alternative to boosting self-esteem and tackles the problem by removing self-rating.

Unconditional self-acceptance means untangling your self-worth from external 'measures' or 'ratings' of your value as a person. Eventually, you can become less likely to consider yourself defective or inadequate on the basis of failures or disapproval, because you view yourself as a *fallible human being*, whose worth remains more or less constant.

Self-acceptance involves making the following assertions:

✔ As a human being, you're a unique, multifaceted individual.

✔ You're ever-changing and developing.

✔ You may be able, to some degree, to measure specific aspects of yourself (such as how tall you are), but you'll never manage to rate the whole of yourself because you're too complex and continuously changing.

✔ Humans, by their very nature, are fallible and imperfect.

✔ By extension, because you're a complex, unique, ever-changing individual, you cannot legitimately be rated or measured as a whole person.

Understanding that you have worth because you're human

Albert Ellis, founder of rational emotive behaviour therapy – one of the very earliest approaches to CBT – states that *all human beings* have *extrinsic* value to others and *intrinsic* value to themselves. But we humans gamely confuse the two and classify ourselves as 'worthy' or 'good' on the basis of assumed value to others. We humans too easily allow our self-worth to be contingent upon the opinions and value judgements of others. Many cognitive behaviour therapists (and indeed other kinds of psychotherapists) hold the implicit value of a human being at the very heart of their perspective.

Imagine how much easier your life will be, and how much more stable your self-esteem will be, if you realise that you have worth as a person *independently* of how much other people value you. You can appreciate being liked, admired or respected without feeling a dire necessity to prompt these responses, or living in fear of losing them.

Appreciating that you're too complex to globally measure or rate

You may mistakenly define your whole worth – or even your entire self – on the basis of your individual parts. Doing so is pointless, because humans are ever-changing, dynamic, fallible and complex creatures.

Humans have the capacity to work on correcting less desirable behaviours and maximising more desirable behaviours. You have the distinctive ability to strive for self-improvement, to maximise your potential and to learn from your and others' histories, mistakes and accomplishments. In short, you have the capacity to develop the ability to accept yourself as you are, while still endeavouring to improve yourself if you so choose.

Letting go of labelling

Self-acceptance means deciding to resist labelling yourself at all and rather to entertain the idea that ratings are inappropriate to the human condition. For example:

✔ You lied to a friend once. Does that make you a liar forever and for all time?

✔ You used to smoke cigarettes but then you decided to give them up. Are you still a smoker because you once smoked?

✔ You failed at one or more tasks that were important to you. Can you legitimately conclude that you are an utter failure?

✔ By the same token, if you succeeded at one important task, are you now a thoroughgoing success?

Take a pack of self-adhesive notes and a large, flat surface. A wall or a door works well – or try a mate if he has a few spare minutes. Write down on one of the notes a characteristic that you, as a whole person, possess; then stick the note on the wall, door or volunteer. Keep doing this, writing down all the aspects of yourself that you can think of until you run out of characteristics, or sticky notes. Now step back and admire your illustration of your complexity as a human being. Appreciate the fact that you cannot legitimately be rated globally.

During the process of accepting yourself, you may experience sadness, disappointment, or remorse for your blunders. These healthy negative emotions may be uncomfortable, but usually they can lead to self-helping, corrective and 'adaptive' behaviours. Self-condemnation or self-depreciation, on the other hand, are likely to lead to far more intense, unhealthy negative emotions, such as depression, hurt, guilt and shame. So, you're more likely to adopt self-defeating, 'maladaptive' behaviours, such as avoidance or giving up.

Forgiving flaws in yourself and others

Interestingly, you may overlook some imperfections in yourself while condemning the same shortcomings in others, or vice versa. To some degree, this relates to what you consider important, your flexibility and your level of self-acceptance. Consider the following scenarios:

✔ Julian works in a computer shop. Whenever he's about to close a sale, he gets excited and trips over some of his words. He feels a bit foolish about this, although none of his customers has ever mentioned it.

✔ Margarita has a poor sense of direction. Sometimes she forgets which way is left and which is right. When she's driving, Margarita has difficulty following directions and frequently finds herself lost.

✔ Carlos is a good student, but has difficulty in exam situations. He studies earnestly but, come the day of the test, he forgets what he's read and performs poorly.

You can't always change things about yourself. Sometimes you can improve a bit, but sometimes you can't change at all. If you're a fully developed adult and five-foot tall, you're unlikely to be able to make yourself grow to six foot through sheer determination. The trick is to begin to recognise where you can make changes and where you can't. Living happily is about accepting your limitations without putting yourself down for them and capitalising on your strengths. So, taking the three examples above:

✔ Julian may be able to make himself less anxious about a potential sale; therefore, he may speak more coherently. By accepting that he mangles his words sometimes, but not condemning himself for it, he may come some way towards overcoming this aspect of his behaviour.

✔ Margarita may simply be someone who's not particularly good at navigation. She may improve with practice, but she may also do well to accept that she's the person who turns up late for parties two streets away from her home.

✔ Carlos can look at his studying habits and see whether he can study more effectively. However, he may simply be someone who does better on practical assignments rather than tests.

Overall, Julian, Carlos and Margarita can choose to accept themselves as fallible human beings and work to improve in the areas described, while also accepting their personal limitations. They can choose to embrace their inherent fallibility as part of the experience of being a human, and understand that their 'less good' traits are part of their individual composition as much as their 'good' traits.

Alternatively, they can choose to evaluate themselves on the basis of their 'less good' traits and judge themselves as worthless, or less than worthy. But where, oh where, do you go from there?

Valuing your uniqueness

Who else do you know who's exactly – and yes, we do mean *exactly* – like you? The correct answer is no one, because the human cloning thing hasn't really taken off yet. So you are, in fact, quite unique – just like everyone else!

You alone are possessor of your own little idiosyncrasies. So learn to laugh it up, because the mistakes and foot-in-mouth moments will just keep on coming, whether you like it or not.

Why self-acceptance beliefs work

At first glance, self-acceptance and self-acceptance beliefs may seem like a tall order or 'not what people think'. However, incorporating self-accepting beliefs into your life can really make a difference in your life, and we recommend it for the following reasons:

✔ **Self-acceptance beliefs are helpful.** You're inspired to correct your poor behaviour or address your shortcomings on the basis that you give yourself permission to be flawed. You allow yourself a margin for error. When problems occur or you behave poorly, you can experience appropriate and proportionate negative emotions and then move on. People are generally more effective problem-solvers when they're not severely emotionally distressed.

✔ **Self-acceptance beliefs are consistent with reality.** Do you know anyone who's entirely flawless?

If you have only conditional self-acceptance, you're subscribing to a belief that you cease to be acceptable, or worthwhile, when you fall short of those conditions or ideals. Basically, you're telling yourself that you must succeed at any given task. Because you can (and do) both fail and succeed, the evidence suggests that your demand to always succeed is erroneous.

✔ **Self-acceptance beliefs are logical.** Just because you *prefer* to behave in a certain way, doesn't mean that you *must* behave in a certain way. Nor does your failing to act in that manner logically render you a failure in all respects. Rather, this 'failure' supports the premise that you're a fallible human capable of behaving in differing ways at various times. To broaden the point, this 'failure' highlights your humanness and your inherent capacity to do both 'well' and 'less well'.

Taking yourself overly seriously is not a successful path to obtaining good mental health. Your individual human fallibility can be both amusing and illuminating. Think about comedy programmes and films. Much of what makes these shows funny is the way the characters *behave*, the mistakes they make, their social blunders, their physicality, their personal peculiarities, and so on. When you laugh at these characters, you aren't being malicious – you just recognise echoes of yourself and of the entire human experience in them. Furthermore, you're unlikely to put down these characters on the basis of their errors. Give yourself a similar benefit of the doubt. Accepting the existence of personal shortcomings can help you to understand your own limitations and identify areas that you may wish to target for change.

Using self-acceptance to aid self-improvement

As we touch upon in the nearby sidebar, which covers accepting flaws in others and yourself, self-acceptance can lead to healthy and *appropriate* negative emotional responses to adverse experiences. This type of emotional response tends to lead to functional or *adaptive* behaviours. Self-denigration, on the other hand, leads to unhealthy, *inappropriate* emotional responses, which in turn tend to produce unhelpful or *destructive* behaviours. Look at the following situation:

> Wendy's been a full-time mum for the past ten years. Before she had her children, she worked as a legal secretary. Now that her children are older, she wants to return to work. Wendy attends a job interview. During the interview, she becomes very nervous and is unable to answer some of the questions adequately. She notices that she's becoming flustered and hot. It also becomes clear to her that secretarial work has evolved in the past ten years and that she lacks the computer skills necessary for the post. Unfortunately, she doesn't get the job.

Now consider two very different responses to the interview:

> **Response A:** Wendy leaves the interview, ruminating on her poor performance all the way home. 'I looked such an idiot,' she tells herself. 'They must have thought me a

real amateur, blushing and stuttering like that. I'm such a failure. Who'd want to hire someone as lacking in skills as me? I don't know what made me think I'd be able to get into work again anyway. I'm clearly not up to standard at all.' Wendy feels depressed and hopeless. She mopes around the house and continues to think about what a failure she is. She feels so ashamed about failing the interview that she avoids talking about it to her friends, thus denying herself the opportunity to receive feedback, which may be useful or help her feel more balanced. Wendy stops looking in the employment pages.

Response B: Wendy leaves the interview and thinks: 'I really didn't present very well in there. I wish I hadn't been so obviously nervous. Clearly, I need to get some computer skills before I'm likely to get a job offer.' Wendy feels very disappointed about not getting the job, but she doesn't conclude that failing one important task makes her a failure. She feels regretful, but not ashamed, about her performance and talks to a few friends about it. Her friends give her some encouragement. Wendy then enrols on an IT course at her local college. She continues to look through the job ads in the paper.

In response B, Wendy is understandably disappointed with how the interview turned out. She's able to recognise her skills' deficit. Because she accepts herself with this *specific deficit*, she takes concrete steps towards improving her skills base.

In response A, Wendy is not thinking about how to do better at the next interview. She's thinking about how she'd like to crawl under the carpet and spend the rest of her days there. A bit of an extreme reaction considering the circumstances, but Wendy isn't considering the circumstances. She's decided that messing up an interview equals total failure, and she's feeling far too depressed and ashamed to start problem-solving.

Generally, your failures and errors aren't as important or calamitous as you think they are. Most of the time, your failures mean a lot more to you than they do to other people.

Understanding that acceptance doesn't mean giving up

In the example of Wendy, we don't suggest that she must resign herself to a life of unemployment simply because she lacks computer skills. Why should she? Clearly, she can do things to ensure that she stands a good chance of getting back into the job market.

In Wendy's case, self-acceptance means that she can view herself as worthwhile, while getting on with self-improvement in specific areas of her life. By contrast, if Wendy refuses to accept herself and puts herself down, she's far more likely to resign – perhaps even condemn – herself to her current state of unemployment.

Resignation requires little or no effort, but self-acceptance can involve a lot of personal effort.

✓ **High frustration tolerance** (HFT) is the ability to tolerate discomfort and hard work in the *short term*, en route to achieving an identified *long-term* goal. In response B in the job interview example, Wendy accepts herself and holds an HFT attitude. She's prepared to do the work necessary to reach her goal of getting a job.

✓ **Low frustration tolerance** (LFT) is unwillingness to tolerate *short-term* pain for *long-term* gain. An LFT attitude is present in statements such as 'It's too difficult to change – this is just the way I am' and 'I may as well just give up'. Resignation and LFT go hand in hand. In Wendy's response A, she refuses to accept herself in view of her recent experience and resigns herself to unemployment.

Resignation may seem like an easier option than self-acceptance because it means that you have to *do* less. However, people tend to feel pretty miserable when they resign and condemn themselves, refusing to put effort into improving their situation.

Being Inspired to Change

You may think that self-acceptance is all fine and well when talking about human error, social gaffes and minor character flaws, but the dice are more loaded in instances where you've transgressed your personal moral code.

If you've behaved in an antisocial, illegal or immoral manner, you may have more difficulty accepting yourself. But you can! Accepting *yourself* doesn't mean accepting the negative behaviour and continuing to do it. On the contrary, accepting yourself involves recognising that you – an acceptable human being – have engaged in a poor, or unacceptable, behaviour. Accepting yourself makes you more likely to learn from your mistakes and act more constructively – which is in both your interest and in those around you.

Consider the following two scenarios:

- ✔ Malcolm has an anger problem. He puts unreasonable demands on his wife and children to never get on his nerves. He has a bad day at work and comes home to find no dinner on the table and his two young children playing noisily in the sitting room. Malcolm shouts at his wife and slaps her. He calls his children names and hits them. His family is afraid and upset. This happens on a regular basis.

- ✔ Fiona works in a shoe shop. She's been stealing money from the till to buy alcohol and codeine-based painkillers. Usually, she takes the tablets throughout the day and drinks heavily in the evenings, until she passes out. Lately, she's called in sick to work more often because she has terrible hangovers and feels very depressed. Fiona often calls herself a 'useless drunk' and 'a low-life thief', and then drinks more to stop herself thinking. She works hard to hide her drinking and stealing, and feels ashamed of herself most of the time.

Are Malcolm and Fiona bad people, or are they just currently exhibiting bad behaviours? If you condemn Malcolm or Fiona – or, indeed, yourself – as a 'bad person' on the basis of bad behaviour, you're missing the point that a person is more complex than a single act.

In order to overcome destructive or socially unacceptable behaviours, you need to do the following:

✔ **Take personal responsibility for your bad behaviour.** Rather than deciding you're just a bad person who has no control or responsibility for your actions, accept that you're doing bad things.

  In the example above, Malcolm's doing very bad things when he takes out his anger on his family. But, if he decides that he's a bad person overall, he relinquishes his responsibility to change. Basically, he's saying: 'I beat my family because I'm a bad person through and through and therefore I can't change.' He's also more likely to attribute his violence to external factors rather than to his own unreasonable demands: 'They know what I'm like and they should damn-well stay out of my way when I come in from work.'

✔ **Identify clearly what you're doing that's wrong or unacceptable.** You must be specific when pinpointing bad behaviours.

  For example, Fiona has two definite serious problems or 'bad' behaviours. First, she has an addiction; second, she's stealing to support that addiction. Fiona's shame and self-condemnation are very likely going to get in the way of her overcoming her problems. She cannot put in the hard work needed to recover from her addiction (which includes seeking professional help) if she can't accept herself as worth the effort.

To move on in life in a way that contributes to the kind of world you'd like to live in, assume personal responsibility and keep working on your self-acceptance.

Actioning Self-Acceptance

Just like virtually all skills worth acquiring, you're going to have to work hard and practise in order to achieve successful self-acceptance skills. This section focuses on ways to start integrating self-acceptance into your daily life.

Self-talking your way to self-acceptance

What's in a name? Rather a lot, actually. As we discuss in Chapters 3 and 8, most people largely *feel* the way they *think*. In other words, the meanings you assign to events have a great deal to do with how you ultimately feel about those events.

Similarly, meaning is attached to the names you call yourself. If you use abusive, harshly critical or profane terminology to give utterance to your behaviours or traits, then you're heading towards emotional disturbance.

The notion that you may start to believe something if you tell yourself it enough times, is partly true. Fortunately, you can *choose* what messages you give yourself and, therefore, choose how you think and feel about yourself.

How you talk to yourself impacts immediately, or obliquely, on your self-concept. Try the following self-talk strategies to make the best impact on yourself:

✔ **Desist with global labels.** Humans often call themselves losers, idiots, failures, stupid or unlovable because of certain events or actions they've been involved in or done.

✔ **Be specific with your self-assessments.** Before you classify yourself as a failure, ask yourself the following questions: 'In what specific way have I failed?' 'In what specific way have I acted stupidly?' It's far less easy to fall into global self-rating when you force yourself to be specific.

✔ **Say what you mean and mean what you say.** You may be saying to yourself right now: 'Oh, but I don't *mean* it when I call myself those bad names.' No? Then don't say them!

Following the best-friend argument

Out of habit, most humans employ double standards: you judge your friends by an entirely different, often more accepting, standard than you use on yourself.

Try to take the same attitude of acceptance towards yourself that you take towards your friends and family. Consider the following:

- **Act like your best friend by judging your behaviour but not judging yourself.** Eustace has been having difficulties in his marriage. He has been staying out late before going home and being verbally abusive to his wife. His best mate, Lucian, has highlighted Eustace's poor behaviour in their conversations but he isn't about to define Eustace as a complete pig on the strength of his arguments with his wife.

- **Accept your failings as you would those of a dear friend.** Laura just failed her driving test for the fourth time. She feels very down about it. Her best friend, Maggie, tells her to try again and to be less hard on herself. Even if Laura never drives, Maggie will likely remain her friend because of other things she likes and appreciates about Laura.

- **View your behaviour within the context of your circumstances, and above all, be compassionate.** Rivka had an abortion following a short affair. She feels very guilty and can't imagine putting the event behind her. Rivka's close friend, Carla, reminds her of the unfortunate circumstances she found herself in at the time, and tells her that she's still someone that she likes and respects very much.

Ask yourself whether the punishment fits the crime. Are you being fair on yourself? What punishment would you dole out to your best friend for the same behaviour? Be aware that you may be making yourself feel extremely guilty, or ashamed, inappropriately.

Dealing with doubts and reservations

Many people feel that, by accepting themselves, they're simply letting themselves off the hook. But self-acceptance is about taking personal responsibility for your less good traits, actions and habits. Self-acceptance is not saying: 'Hey, I'm human and fallible! Therefore, I just am the way I am and I don't need to think about changing anything.' Self-acceptance is about targeting areas that you both *can* and *wish to* change and then taking the appropriate steps towards change.

Imperfect self-acceptance

As you're a fallible human being, you won't be perfect at self-acceptance either. You'll very probably slip into putting yourself down from time to time, as everyone does – us included. The aim is to accept yourself more often and to accept yourself again more quickly, if you notice that you're putting yourself down. Such acceptance definitely gets easier and more consistent with practice.

Broadly speaking, you may be using one of two common strategies to manage low self-esteem: avoiding doing things, or doing things excessively. For example, a person who believes they're worthless unless they're liked by everybody may try extra hard to avoid rejection or to win people's approval; while a person who regards themselves as a 'failure' may try to avoid situations in which they might fail.

Part IV
Looking Backwards and Moving Forwards

The 5th Wave   By Rich Tennant

"My hunch, Mr. Pesko, is that you're still making mountains out of mole hills."

In this part . . .

*P*utting your present problems into context based on your past experiences is central to CBT, and this part helps you to do just that. You'll also find information on how to consolidate new ways of thinking, as well as tips about making productive behavioural changes stick. We'll help you to overcome common obstacles to positive change and show you how to get and best use professional help.

Chapter 11

Taking a Fresh Look at Your Past

*Y*our past experiences have an effect on how you think and function now. Sometimes, you may endure bad experiences and be able to make some good things happen from them. At other times, you may be wounded by unpleasant events and carry that injury with you into your present and future.

This chapter encourages you to examine openly whether your past experiences have led you to develop *core beliefs* that may be causing your current emotional difficulties.

People are sometimes surprised to find out that CBT considers the past an important aspect of understanding one's problems. Unlike traditional Freudian psychoanalysis, which focuses intensively on childhood relationships and experiences, CBT specifically investigates past experiences in order to see how these early events may still be affecting people in their *present* lives.

Exploring How Your Past Can Influence Your Present

We don't know what your childhood and early adulthood were like, but many people share relatively common past experiences. The following examples highlight various aspects of past experience that may resonate with your life history. Rather than focusing on the differences between these examples and your own experiences, use the examples to identify similar things that have happened to you in your own life.

- ✔ Sybil grew up with parents who fought a lot. She learnt to be very quiet and to keep out of the way so that her parents' anger wouldn't be directed at her. She always tried to be a very good girl and no trouble to anyone.

- ✔ Rashid had critical parents. The demands Rashid's parents made of him to be a 'high achiever' made it clear to him that he would get their love and approval only when he did well in sports and at school.

- ✔ Beth had a violent father who would frequently beat her and other family members when he was in a bad mood. At other times, her father was very loving and funny. Beth could never predict accurately what mood her father would be in when he came through the front door.

- ✔ Milo's relationships have never lasted for very long. Most of the women he's dated have been unfaithful to him. Milo's partners often complain that he's too insecure and suspicious of their friendships with members of the opposite sex.

- ✔ Mahesh lost his oldest son and the family business in a fire five years ago. His wife has been depressed since the fire, and their marriage seems to be falling apart. Recently, his teenage daughter has been in trouble with the police. No one seems to offer Mahesh support. He feels dogged by bad luck.

Many other different kinds of difficult experiences can contribute to the development of negative core beliefs:

- ✔ Death of loved ones

- ✔ Growing up with neglectful, critical or abusive parents or siblings

✔ Divorce

✔ Being bullied at school

✔ Being abandoned by a parent or significant other

✔ Undergoing a trauma, such as rape, life-threatening illness, accidents or witnessing violent attacks on other people

These are just some examples of the types of event that can have a profound effect on mental health generally. Negative events that contribute to the way you think about yourself, other people and the world often occur in childhood or early adult life. However, events occurring at any stage of your life can have a significant impact on the way you think about the world.

Identifying Your Core Beliefs

Your *core beliefs* are ideas or philosophies that you hold very strongly and very deeply. These ideas are usually developed in childhood or early in adult life. Core beliefs can be both positive and negative. Good experiences of life and of other people generally lead to the development of healthy ideas about yourself, other people and the world. In this chapter we deal with negative core beliefs because these are the types of belief that cause people's emotional problems.

Sometimes, the negative core beliefs that are formed during childhood can be reinforced by later experiences, which seem to confirm their validity.

For example, one of Beth's core beliefs is 'I'm bad'. She develops this belief to make sense of her father beating her for no real or obvious reason. Later, Beth has a few experiences of being punished unreasonably by teachers at school, which reinforce her belief in her 'badness'.

Core beliefs are characteristically global and absolute, like Beth's 'I'm bad'. People hold core beliefs to be 100 per cent true under all conditions. You often form your core beliefs when you're a child to help you make sense of your childhood experiences, and so you may never evaluate whether your core beliefs are the best way to make sense of your adult experiences. As an adult, you may continue to act, think and feel as though the core beliefs of your childhood are still 100 per cent true.

Your core beliefs are called 'core' because they're your deeply held ideas and they're at the very centre of your belief system. Core beliefs give rise to rules, demands or assumptions, which in turn produce *automatic thoughts* (thoughts that just pop into your head when you're confronted with a situation). You can think of these three layers of beliefs as a dartboard with core beliefs as the bull's-eye. Figure 11-1 shows the interrelationship between the three layers, and shows the assumptions and automatic thoughts that surround Beth's core belief that she's bad.

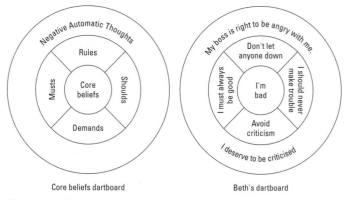

Core beliefs dartboard   Beth's dartboard

Figure 11-1: The core beliefs dartboard and Beth's dartboard, showing the three layers of beliefs.

Another way of describing a core belief is as a lens or filter, through which you interpret all the information you receive from other people and the world around you.

The three camps of core beliefs

Core beliefs fall into three main camps: beliefs about yourself, beliefs about other people, and beliefs about the world.

Beliefs about yourself

Unhelpful negative core beliefs about yourself often have their roots in damaging early experiences. Being bullied or ostracised at school, or experiencing neglect, abuse or harsh criticism from caregivers, teachers or siblings can inform the way in which you understand yourself.

For example, Beth's experiences of physical abuse led her to form the core belief 'I'm bad'.

Beliefs about other people

Negative core beliefs about others often develop as a result of traumatic incidents involving other people. A traumatic incident can mean personal harm inflicted on you by another person or witnessing harm being done to others. Negative core beliefs can also develop from repeated negative experiences with other people, such as teachers and parents.

For example, because Beth's father was violent and abusive towards her but also could be funny when he wanted to be, she developed a core belief that 'people are dangerous and unpredictable'.

Beliefs about the world

People who've experienced trauma, lived with severe deprivation or survived in harmful, insecure, unpredictable environments are prone to forming negative core beliefs about life and the world.

Beth holds a core belief – that 'the world is full of bad things' – which she developed as a result of her early home situation and events at school later on.

Sometimes, core beliefs from all three camps are taught to you explicitly as a child. Your parents or caregivers may have given you *their* core beliefs. For example, you may have been taught that 'life's cruel and unfair' before you have any experiences that lead you to form such a belief yourself.

How your core beliefs interact

Identifying core beliefs about yourself can help you to understand why you keep having the same problems. However, if you can also get to know your fundamental beliefs about other people and the world, you can build a fuller picture of why some situations distress you. For example, Beth may find being yelled at by her boss depressing because it fits with her core belief 'I'm bad', but the experience also seems to confirm her belief that people are unpredictable and aggressive.

Like many people, you may hold core beliefs that you're unlovable, unworthy or inadequate – these beliefs are about your basic worth, goodness or value. Or perhaps you hold beliefs about your capability to look after yourself or to cope with adversity – these beliefs are about how helpless or powerful you are in relation to other people and the world.

Mahesh, for example, may believe 'I'm helpless' because he's experienced tragedy and a lot of bad luck. He may also hold beliefs that 'the world is against me' and 'other people are uncaring'. Looking at these three beliefs together, you can see why Mahesh is feeling depressed.

Detecting Your Core Beliefs

Because core beliefs are held deeply, you may not think of them or 'hear' them as clear statements in your head. You're probably much more aware of your negative automatic thoughts or your rules than you are of your core beliefs.

The following sections show you some methods you can use to really get to the root of your belief system.

Following a downward arrow

One technique to help you pinpoint your problematic core beliefs is the *downward arrow* method, which involves you identifying a situation that causes you to have an unhealthy negative emotion, such as depression or guilt. (For more on healthy and unhealthy negative emotions, check out Chapter 5.)

After you've identified a situation that brings up negative emotions, ask yourself what the situation means or says about you. Your first answer is probably your *negative automatic thought* (NAT). Keep asking yourself what your previous answer means or says about you until you reach a global, absolute statement, such as 'other people are dangerous' or 'I'm bad' in Beth's case.

For example, when Rashid uses the downward arrow method to examine his feelings about failing a university entrance exam, he has the negative automatic thought:

NAT: 'I'll never get into a good university.'

What does this NAT mean about me?

'I've disappointed my parents again.'

What does disappointing my parents mean about me?

'Every time I try to do well at something, I fail.'

What does failing mean about me?

'I'm a failure.' (Rashid's core belief)

You can use the same downward arrow technique to get to your core beliefs about other people and the world. Just keep asking yourself what your NAT *means about others or the world*. Ultimately, you can end up with a conclusive statement that is your core belief. The following is an example of how to do this, using the situation of getting a parking ticket:

NAT: 'These kinds of things are always happening to me.'

What does this mean about the world?

'Bad things are always just around the corner.'

What does this mean about the world?

'The world is full of tragedy and hardship.'

What does this mean about the world?

'Life is against me.' (Core belief)

Picking up clues from your dreaming and screaming

Imagine your worst nightmare. Think of dream scenarios that wake you up screaming. Somewhere in these terrifying scenarios may be one or more of your core beliefs. Some examples of core beliefs that can show themselves in dreams and nightmares include:

- Drying up while speaking publicly
- Being rejected by your partner for another person
- Being criticised in front of work colleagues
- Getting lost in a foreign country
- Hurting someone's feelings
- Doing something thoughtless and being picked up on it
- Letting down someone important in your life
- Being controlled by another person
- Being at someone else's mercy

Look for the similarities between your nightmare scenarios and situations that upset you in real life. Ask yourself what a dreaded dream situation may mean about yourself, about other people or about the world. Keep considering what each of your answers means about yourself, others or the world until you reach a core belief.

Tracking themes

Another way of journeying to the core of your core beliefs is to look for themes in your automatic thoughts. A good way of doing this is by reviewing your completed ABC forms (which we describe in Chapter 3).

For example, if you find that you often have thoughts related to failure, getting things wrong or being less capable than other people, you may have a core belief of 'I'm inadequate' or 'I'm incompetent'.

Filling in the blanks

Another method of eliciting your core beliefs is simply to fill in the blanks. Take a piece of paper, write the following, and fill in the blanks:

I am _____

Other people are _____

The world is _____

This method requires you to take almost a wild guess about what your core beliefs are. Ultimately, you're in a better position than anyone else to take a guess, so the exercise is worth a shot.

You can review written work that you've done, which is a good technique for discovering your core beliefs. Going over what you've written again enables you to refine, tweak or alter your beliefs. Be sure to use language that represents how you truly speak to yourself. Core beliefs are very idiosyncratic. However you choose to articulate them is entirely up to you. The same is true of the healthy alternative beliefs you develop (see the 'Developing Alternatives to Your Core Beliefs' section, later in this chapter). Make sure that you put alternative beliefs into language that reflects the way that you speak to yourself.

Understanding the Impact of Core Beliefs

Core beliefs are your fundamental and enduring ways of perceiving and making sense of yourself, the world and other people. Your core beliefs have been around since early in your life. These core beliefs are so typically engrained and unconscious that you're probably not aware of their impact on your emotions and behaviours.

Spotting when you are acting according to old beliefs

People tend to behave according to the beliefs they hold about themselves, others and the world. To evaluate whether your core beliefs are unhealthy, you need to pay attention to your corresponding behaviours. Unhealthy core beliefs typically lead to problematic behaviours.

For example, Milo believes that he's unlovable and that other people cannot be trusted. Therefore, he tends to be passive with his girlfriends, to seek reassurance that they're not about to leave him, and to become suspicious and jealous of their interactions with other men. Often, Milo's girlfriends get fed up with his jealousy and insecurity and end the relationship.

Because Milo operates according to his core belief about being unlovable, he behaves in ways that actually tend to drive his partners away from him. Milo doesn't yet see that his core belief, and corresponding insecurity, is what causes problems in his relationships. Instead, Milo views each time a partner leaves him for someone else as further evidence that his core belief of 'I'm unlovable' is true.

Sybil believes that she mustn't draw attention to herself because one of her core beliefs is 'other people are likely to turn on me'. Therefore, she's quiet in social situations and is reluctant to assert herself. Her avoidant, self-effacing behaviour means that she doesn't often get what she wants, which feeds her core belief 'I'm unimportant'.

Sybil acts in accordance with her core belief that other people are likely to turn on her and, subsequently, deprives herself of the opportunity to see that this is not always going to happen. If Sybil and Milo identify their negative core beliefs, they can begin to develop healthier new beliefs and behaviours that can yield better results. We look more closely at how to develop new, more positive core beliefs later in this chapter.

Seeing that unhealthy core beliefs make you prejudiced

When you begin to examine your core beliefs, it may seem to you that everything in your life is conspiring to make your unhealthy core belief ring true. More than likely, your core belief is leading you to take a prejudiced view of all your experiences. Unhealthy beliefs, such as 'I'm unlovable' and 'other people are dangerous', distort the way in which you process information. Negative information that supports your unhealthy belief is let in. Positive information that contradicts the negative stuff is either rejected, or twisted to mean something negative in keeping with your unhealthy belief.

The prejudice model in Figure 11-2 shows you how your unhealthy core beliefs can reject positive events that may *contradict* them. At the same time, your core beliefs can collect negative events that may *support* their validity. Your unhealthy core beliefs can also lead you to distort positive events into negative events so that they continue to make your beliefs seem true.

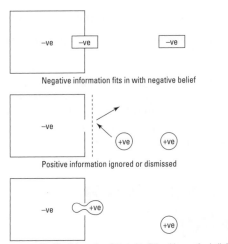

Negative information fits in with negative belief

Positive information ignored or dismissed

Positive information distorted to fit in with negative belief

Figure 11-2: The prejudice model illustrates how you sometimes distort positive information to fit in with your negative core beliefs.

For example, here's how Beth's core belief 'I'm bad' causes her to prejudice her experiences:

- ✔ **Negative experience:** Beth's boss is angry about a missed deadline, affirming her belief that 'I'm bad'.

- ✔ **Positive experience:** Beth's boss is happy about the quality of her report, which Beth distorts as 'he's happy about this report only because all my other work is such rubbish', further affirming her belief that 'I'm bad'.

Beth also ignores smaller *positive* events that don't support her belief that she's bad, such as:

- ✔ People seem to like her at work.

- ✔ Co-workers tell her that she's conscientious at work.

- ✔ Her friends telephone her and invite her out.

However, Beth is quick to take notice of smaller *negative* events that do seem to match up with her belief that she's bad, for example:

✔ Someone pushes her rudely on a busy train.

✔ Her boyfriend shouts at her during an argument.

✔ A work colleague doesn't smile at her when she enters the office.

Beth's core belief of 'I'm bad' acts as a filter through which all her experiences are interpreted. It basically stops her from re-evaluating herself as anything other than bad; it makes her prejudiced against herself. This is why identifying negative core beliefs and targeting them for change is so important!

Making a Formulation of Your Beliefs

When you've identified your core beliefs using the techniques outlined in the previous sections, you can use the form in Figure 11-3 to make a formulation of your beliefs and rules. Filling out this form gives you an 'at a glance' reference of what your negative core beliefs are and how they lead you to act in unhelpful ways. The form is a handy reminder of the beliefs you need to target for change and why.

Follow these steps to fill out the form:

1. **Relevant Early/Past Experiences. In this box, write down any significant past events that you think may have contributed to the development of your specific negative core beliefs.**

   For example, Beth records:

   • Father was physically abusive and had unpredictable mood swings

   • Father told me that I was bad

   • I received severe and unreasonable punishment from teachers

FORMULATION OF MY BELIEFS AND RULES

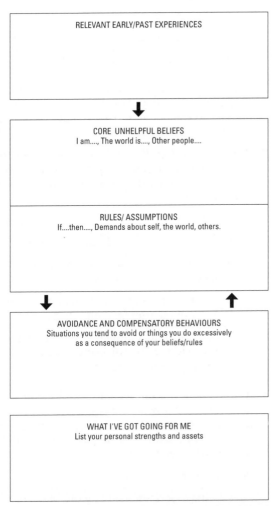

RELEVANT EARLY/PAST EXPERIENCES

CORE UNHELPFUL BELIEFS
I am...., The world is...., Other people....

RULES/ ASSUMPTIONS
If....then...., Demands about self, the world, others.

AVOIDANCE AND COMPENSATORY BEHAVIOURS
Situations you tend to avoid or things you do excessively
as a consequence of your beliefs/rules

WHAT I'VE GOT GOING FOR ME
List your personal strengths and assets

Figure 11-3: Make a formulation of your beliefs with the help of this form.

2. **Core ('Unconditional') Unhelpful Beliefs. Write your identified core beliefs about yourself, other people and the world in this box.**

Beth records her beliefs like this:

- I am bad
- Other people are unpredictable and dangerous
- The world is full of bad things

The word 'unconditional' is used on this form to remind you that core beliefs are those beliefs that you hold to be 100 per cent true, 100 per cent of the time, and under any conditions.

3. **Rules/'Conditional' Beliefs. In this box write down the rules or demands you place on yourself, other people and the world *because of* your core negative beliefs.**

Beth writes:

- I must be 'good' at all times (demand on self).
- *If* I am criticised *then* it means that I'm a bad person (conditional rule).
- Other people must not find fault with me or think badly of me (demand on others).
- The world must not conspire to remind me of how bad I am by throwing negative experiences my way (demand on the world).

4. **Avoidance and Compensatory Behaviours. Use this box to record how you try to avoid triggering your negative core beliefs, or unhelpful things you do to try to cope with your negative core beliefs when they're triggered.**

Beth records:

- Being a perfectionist at work in order to avoid any criticism
- Avoiding confrontation and thereby not asserting myself at work or with friends
- Over-apologising when I do get criticised or make a small mistake
- Always assuming that other people's opinions are 'right' and that my own opinions are 'wrong'

- Being timid in social situations to avoid being noticed

- Not trusting others and assuming that they're ultimately going to hurt me somehow

5. **What I've got going for me. Write down positive things about yourself that fly in the face of your negative core beliefs.**

Beth writes:

- My work colleagues seem to like me.

- I am very conscientious at work and this has been commented on by my boss and by colleagues.

- I have some good friends who are trustworthy.

- There have been some good things that have happened to me, such as finishing college and getting a good job.

- I am generally hardworking and honest.

- I care about other people's feelings and opinions.

Information you write down in this box is important because it can be used to help you develop more balanced and helpful alternative core beliefs. (We explain more about how to construct healthy core beliefs in the following sections.)

Limiting the Damage: Being Aware of Core Beliefs

To reduce the negative impact of your unhelpful core beliefs, try to get better at spotting the beliefs being activated. Step back and consider a more unbiased explanation for events rather than getting swept along by the beliefs.

One way of improving your awareness of your core beliefs is to develop a *core belief flashcard*. This written-down statement includes the following:

✔ What your core belief is.

✔ How your core belief affects the way you interpret events.

✔ How you tend to act when the core belief is triggered.

✔ What a more unbiased interpretation of events is likely to be.

✔ What alternative behaviour may be more productive.

For example, Sybil wrote the following core belief flashcard:

> When my core belief of 'I'm unimportant' is triggered, I'm probably taking something personally and wanting to withdraw. Instead, I can remember that most people don't hold this view of me, and then I can stay engaged in the social situation.

Carry your flashcard around with you and review it often, even several times a day. Use your flashcard, especially when you notice that your core belief has *been* triggered, or just before you enter a situation where you know that your old core belief is *likely* to be triggered.

Developing Alternative Beliefs

When you've put your finger on your core beliefs and identified those that are negative and unhealthy, you're in a position to develop healthier alternative beliefs.

Your new core belief doesn't need to be the extreme opposite of your old belief. Changing an extreme belief such as 'I'm unlovable' to 'I'm lovable' may be too difficult when you're just starting out. Instead, cut yourself some slack and realise that simply by beginning to understand that an unhealthy core belief is not 100 per cent true all of the time is enough. Here are some examples:

✔ Beth's alternative to her unhealthy belief 'I'm bad' is 'there are good things about me'.

✔ Rashid replaces his unhealthy belief 'I'm a failure' with 'I succeed at some things'.

✔ Mahesh chooses the alternative 'good things do happen in the world' to replace his old belief 'the world's against me'.

> ✔ Sybil replaces her belief 'other people will turn against me' with the healthier belief 'many people can be kind'.

> ✔ Milo substitutes his old core belief 'I'm unlovable' with the more accurate belief 'some people do like me, and some people will love me'.

Generating alternatives for your unhealthy and absolute core beliefs is not about positive thinking or platitudes, but is about generating less absolute, more accurate, more realistic opinions about yourself, other people and the world around you.

Revisiting history

Many people can look back over their lives and get a fairly clear picture of where their core beliefs have come from. Sometimes, though, the source of core beliefs is not so clear.

Although most core beliefs arise from your early experiences, you can still form deep entrenched ideas about yourself, life and other people when you're older. For example, Mahesh develops his core beliefs about the world being against him following a string of bad luck and tragic events during his adult years.

Revisit your history with a view to coming up with some reasons behind the ways that you think and behave in the present. Be compassionate with yourself, but recognise that you're the only one who can retrain your brain into updated and healthier ways of understanding your experiences.

Replacing old meanings with new meanings

Experiences that you had earlier on in life were given a meaning by you at the time. As an adult, you're in the fortunate position of being able to reassess the meanings you originally gave certain events and to assign more sophisticated meanings where appropriate.

For example, Beth forms the belief 'I'm bad' based on the information she had when her father was abusing her. She was young and worked on various assumptions, including:

> ✔ Daddy tells me that I've been bad, and this must be true.

> ✔ You get punished when you're bad.

> ✔ I must've done something bad to deserve this treatment.

Now that she's no longer a child and recognises that she has this core belief, Beth can choose to look at her father's abuse and assign different meanings to his treatment of her:

✔ My father had an anger problem that had nothing to do with me.

✔ No child should be punished so severely, no matter how disobedient they've been.

✔ My father was wrong to beat me, and I didn't deserve to be beaten.

✔ My father did a bad thing by beating me and his bad behaviour doesn't mean that I am bad.

Use a three-column old meaning/new meaning worksheet like the one in Table 11-1 to review past events that contributed to the development of your core beliefs and reinterpret them now as an older, wiser person.

The sheet has three headings. Fill them in as follows:

1. **In the first column, 'Event', record what actually happened.**

2. **Under 'Old Meaning' in the second column, record what you believe the event means about you.**

   This is your unhealthy core belief.

3. **In the 'New Meaning' third column, record a healthier and more accurate meaning for the event.**

   This is the new belief that you want to strengthen.

Table 11-1 shows an example of Beth's worksheet.

Table 11-1 Beth's Old Meaning–New Meaning Worksheet

Event	Old Meaning	New Meaning
My Dad yelling, telling me I was bad when I was little.	I must be bad for him to say this so often.	I was much too young and afraid to be 'bad'. It was my father's anger that was the problem.

Incorporating new beliefs into your life

Constructing newer, healthier, more accurate core beliefs is one thing, but beginning to live by them is another. Before your new beliefs are really stuck in your head and heart, you need to act *as if* they're already there. For Beth, this may mean her forcing herself to face up to criticism from her boss and making appropriate adjustments to her work without berating herself. In short, she needs to act *as if* she truly believes that there are good things about herself, even in the face of negative feedback. She needs to operate under the assumption that her boss's anger is a reasonable (or possibly an unreasonable) response to an aspect of her work, rather than proof of her intrinsic badness.

In Chapter 12, we suggest several techniques for strengthening new alternative beliefs.

Starting from scratch

We won't tell you that changing your core beliefs is easy, because that simply isn't true. In fact, erasing your old belief systems is so difficult that we think the best way of dealing with them is to make alternative healthy beliefs stronger so that they can do battle with your unhealthy beliefs.

Think of your old beliefs as well-trodden paths through an overgrown field. You can walk quickly and easily down these paths, as they've been worn down from years of use. Developing new, alternative beliefs is like making new paths through the field. At first, the new paths are awkward and uncomfortable to walk on, because you need to break down the undergrowth.

You may be tempted to walk along the old paths because they're easier and more well-known, but with practice, your new paths can become familiar and natural to walk along. Similarly, with regular practice, thinking and acting along the lines of your alternative beliefs can become stronger and more automatic, even when the going gets tough!

Thinking about what you'd teach a child

When you're challenging your negative core beliefs, try to think about what you'd tell a child. Act as your own parent by reinstructing yourself to endorse healthy ways of viewing others, yourself and the world.

Ask yourself what types of belief you'd teach a child. Would you encourage him to grab hold of the negative core beliefs that you may hold about yourself, or would you want him to think of himself in a more positive and accepting way? Would you wish for him to think of other people as evil, untrustworthy, dangerous and more powerful than himself? Or would you rather he had a more balanced view of people, such as variable but basically okay, generally trustworthy and reliable? Would you want him to believe that he can stand up for himself?

Considering what you'd want a friend to believe

When challenging your core beliefs, think about having a friend like Mahesh, Beth, Rashid, Milo or Sybil. What advice would you give them? Would you say 'Yes, Rashid, you're a failure'? 'I agree, Mahesh – life's against you'? 'Beth, you're bad'? Or would you be quietly horrified to spout these unhealthy and damaging beliefs? We assume the latter.

If you wouldn't want your dear friends to believe such things, why believe them yourself? Talk to yourself like you would to your best friend when your negative core beliefs are activated.

Chapter 12

Moving New Beliefs from Your Head to Your Heart

. . . .

In This Chapter

▶ Strengthening your new, helpful attitudes and beliefs

▶ Dealing with doubts about a new way of thinking

▶ Testing out your new ways of thinking in difficult situations

▶ Preparing for setbacks

. . . .

*A*fter you've identified your unhelpful patterns of thinking and developed more helpful attitudes (see Chapters 2, 3, 10 and 11), you need to reinforce your new thoughts and beliefs. The process of reinforcing new beliefs is like trying to give up a bad habit and develop a good habit in its place. You need to work at making your new, healthy ways of thinking second nature, at the same time as eroding your old ways of thinking. This chapter describes some simple exercises to help you develop and nurture your new beliefs.

In many ways, *integrating* your new method of thinking with your mind, emotions and actions is *the* critical process in CBT. A parrot can repeat rational philosophies, but it doesn't understand or *believe* what it's saying. The real work in CBT is turning intellectual understanding into something you that know in your gut to be true.

Defining the Beliefs You Want to Strengthen

Many people who work at changing their attitudes and beliefs complain: 'I know what I *should* think, but I don't believe it!' When you begin to adopt a new way of thinking, you may *know* that something makes sense but you may not *feel* that the new belief is true.

When you're in a state of *cognitive dissonance* you know that your old way of thinking isn't 100 per cent right, but you aren't yet convinced of the alternative. Being in a state of cognitive dissonance can be uncomfortable because things don't feel quite right. However, this feeling is a good sign that things are changing.

In CBT, we often call this disconnection between thinking and truly believing the *head-to-heart problem*. Basically, you know that an argument is true in your head, but you don't feel it in your heart. For example, if you've spent many years believing that you're less worthy than others or that you need the approval of other people in order to approve of yourself, you may have great difficulty *internalising* (believing in your gut) an alternative belief. You may find that the idea that you have as much basic human worth as the next person, or that approval from others is a bonus but not a necessity, difficult to buy.

Your alternative beliefs are likely to be about three key areas:

- ✔ Yourself
- ✔ Other people
- ✔ The world

Alternative beliefs may take the following formats:

- ✔ A *flexible preference*, instead of a rigid demand or rule, such as 'I'd very much prefer to be loved by my parents, but there's no reason they absolutely *have* to love me.'

- ✔ An *alternative assumption*, which is basically an if/then statement, such as '*If* I don't get an A in my test, *then* that won't be the end of the world. I can still move on in my academic career.'

✔ A *global belief*, which expresses a positive healthy general truth, such as 'I'm basically okay' rather than 'I'm worthless', or 'The world's a place with some safe and some dangerous parts' instead of 'The world's a dangerous place'.

When you do experience the head-to-heart problem, we recommend acting *as if* you really do hold the new belief to be true – we explain how to do this in the following section.

One of your main aims in CBT, after you've developed a more helpful alternative belief, is to increase how strongly you endorse your new belief or raise your *strength of conviction* (SOC). You can rate how much you believe in an alternative healthy philosophy on a 0–100 percentage scale, 0 representing a total lack of conviction and 100 representing an absolute conviction.

Acting As If You Already Believe

You don't need to believe your new philosophy entirely in order to start changing your behaviour. Starting out, it's enough to *know* in your head that your new belief makes sense and then *act* according to your new belief or philosophy. If you consistently do the 'acting as if' technique, which we explain here, your conviction in your new way of thinking is likely to grow over time.

You can use the 'acting as if' technique to consolidate any new way of thinking, in pretty much any situation. Ask yourself the following questions:

✔ How would I behave if I truly considered my new belief to be true?

✔ How would I overcome situational challenges to my new belief if I truly considered it to be true and helpful?

✔ What sort of behaviour would I expect to see in other people who truly endorse this new belief?

You can make a list of your answers to the above questions and refer to it before, after and even during an experience of using the 'acting as if' technique. For example, if you're dealing with social anxiety and trying to get to grips with self-acceptance beliefs, use the 'acting as if' techniques that follow, and ask yourself similar kinds of questions, such as:

✔ **Act consistently with the new belief:** If I truly believed that I was as worthy as anyone else, how would I behave in a social situation?

Be specific about how you'd enter a room, the conversation you may initiate, and what your body language would be like.

✔ **Troubleshoot for challenges to your new belief:** If I truly believed that I was as worthy as anyone else, how would I react to any social hiccups?

Again, be specific about how you may handle lulls in conversation and moments of social awkwardness.

✔ **Observe other people.** Does anyone else in the social situation seem to be acting as if they truly endorse the belief that I'm trying to adopt?

If so, note how the person acts and how they handle awkward silences and normal breaks in conversation. Imitate their behaviour.

When you act in accordance with a new way of thinking or a specific belief, you reinforce the truth of that belief. The more you experience a belief *in action*, the more you can appreciate its beneficial effects on your emotions. In essence, you're rewiring your brain to think in a more helpful and realistic way. Give this technique a try, even if you think that it's wishful thinking or seems silly. Actions do speak louder than words. So if a new belief makes sense to you, follow it up with action.

Building a Portfolio of Arguments

When an old belief rears its ugly head, try to have on hand some strong arguments to support your new belief. Your old beliefs or thinking habits have probably been with you a long time, and they can be tough to shift. You can expect to argue with yourself about the truth and benefit of your new thinking several times before the new stuff well and truly replaces the old.

Your portfolio of arguments can consist of a collection of several arguments against your old way of thinking and several arguments in support of your new way of thinking. You can refer to your portfolio anytime that you feel conviction in your new belief is beginning to wane. Get yourself a small notebook to use as your portfolio of arguments. The following sections help to guide you towards developing sound rationales in support of helpful beliefs and in contradiction of unhelpful beliefs.

Generating arguments against an unhelpful belief

To successfully combat unhealthy beliefs, try the following exercise. At the top of a sheet of paper, write down an old, unhelpful belief you want to weaken. For example, you may write: 'I have to get approval from significant others, such as my boss. Without approval, I'm worthless.' Then, consider the following questions to highlight the unhelpful nature of your belief:

✓ **Is the belief untrue or inconsistent with reality?** Try to find evidence that your belief isn't factually accurate (or at least not 100 per cent accurate for 100 per cent of the time). For example, you don't *have* to get approval from your boss: the universe permits otherwise, and you can survive without such approval. Furthermore, you cannot be defined as worthless on the strength of this experience, because you're much too complex to be defined.

Considering why a certain belief is *understandable* can help you to explain why you hold a particular belief to be true. For example, 'It's understandable that I think I'm stupid because my father often told me I was when I was young, but that was really due to his impatience and his own difficult childhood. So, it follows that I believe myself to be stupid because of my childhood experiences, and not because there's any real truth in the idea that I'm stupid. Therefore, the belief that I'm stupid is consistent with my upbringing but inconsistent with reality.'

✔ **Is the belief rigid?** Consider whether your belief is flexible enough to allow you to adapt to reality. For example, the idea that you *must* get approval or that you *need* approval in order to think well of yourself, is overly rigid. It is entirely possible that you will fail to get approval from significant others at some stage in your life. Unless you have a flexible belief about getting approval, you're destined to think badly of yourself whenever approval isn't forthcoming. Replace the word *must* with *prefer* in this instance, and turn your demand for approval into a flexible preference for approval.

✔ **Is the belief extreme?** Consider whether your unhelpful belief is extreme. For example, equating being disliked by one person with worthlessness is an extreme conclusion. It's rather like concluding that being late for one appointment means that you'll always be late for every appointment you have for the rest of your life. The conclusion that you draw from one or more experiences is far too extreme to accurately reflect reality.

✔ **Is the belief illogical?** Consider whether your belief actually makes sense. You may want approval from your boss, but logically she doesn't *have* to approve of you. Not getting approval from someone significant doesn't logically lead to you being less worthy. Rather, not getting approval shows that you've failed to get approval on this occasion, from this specific person.

✔ **Is the belief unhelpful?** Consider how your belief may or may not be helping you. For example, if you worry about whether your boss is approving of you, you'll probably be anxious at work much of the time. You may feel depressed if your boss treats you with indifference or visibly disapproves of your work. So, is worrying about your boss's approval helpful? Clearly not!

Running through the preceding list of questions is definitely an exercise that involves putting pen to paper or fingertips to keyboard. Try to pick out your unhelpful beliefs and to formulate helpful alternatives, then generate as many watertight arguments against your old belief and in support of your new belief as you can.

Generating arguments to support your helpful alternative belief

The guidelines for generating sound arguments to support alternative, more helpful ways of thinking about yourself, other people and the world, are similar to those suggested in the preceding section, 'Generating arguments against an unhelpful belief'.

On a sheet of paper, write down a helpful alternative belief that you want to use to replace a negative, unhealthy view you hold. For example, a helpful alternative belief regarding approval at work may be: 'I want approval from significant others, such as my boss, but I don't *need* it. If I don't get approval, I still have worth as a person.'

Next, develop arguments to support your alternative belief. Ask yourself the following questions to ensure that your helpful alternative belief is strong and effective:

- ✔ **Is the belief true and consistent with reality?** For example, you really can want approval and fail to get it sometimes. Just because you want something very much doesn't mean to say you'll get it. Lots of people don't get approval from their bosses, but it doesn't mean they're lesser people.

- ✔ **Is the belief flexible?** Consider whether your belief allows you to adapt to reality. For example, the idea that you *prefer* to get approval but that it isn't a dire necessity for either survival or self-esteem, allows for the possibility of not getting approval from time to time. You don't have to form any extreme conclusions about your overall worth in the face of occasions of disapproval.

- ✔ **Is the belief balanced?** Consider whether your helpful belief is balanced and non-extreme. For example, 'Not being liked by my boss is unfortunate but it's not proof of whether I'm worthwhile as a person.' This balanced and flexible belief recognises that disapproval from your boss is undesirable and may mean that you need to reassess your work performance. However, this recognition doesn't hurl you into depression based on the unbalanced belief that you're unworthy for failing to please your boss on this occasion.

✔ **Is the belief logical and sensible?** Show how your alternative belief follows logically from the facts, or from your preferences. It follows logically that your boss's disapproval about one aspect of your work is undesirable and may mean that you need to work harder or differently. It does not follow logically that because of her disapproval you're an overall bad or worthless person.

✔ **Is the belief helpful?** When you accept that you want approval from your boss but that you don't *have* to get it, you can be less anxious about the possibility of incurring your boss's disapproval or failing to make a particular impression. You also stand a better chance of making a good impression at work when you prefer, but are not desperate for, approval. You can be more focused on the job that you're doing and less preoccupied by what your boss may be thinking about you.

Imagine you're about to go into court to present to the jury arguments in defence of your new belief. Develop as many good arguments that support your new belief as you can. Most people find that listing lots of ways in which the new belief is helpful makes the most impact.

Understanding That Practice Makes Imperfect

Despite your best efforts, you may continue to think in rigid and extreme ways and experience unhealthy emotions from time to time. Why? Well, – oh yes, we say it again – you're only human.

Practising your new, healthy ways of thinking and putting them to regular use minimises your chances of relapse. However, you're never going to become a perfectly healthy thinker – humans seem to have a tendency to develop thinking errors and you need a high degree of diligence to resist unhelpful and unhealthy thinking.

Be wary of having a perfectionist attitude about your thinking. You're setting yourself up to fail if you expect that you can always be healthy in thought, emotion and behaviour. Give yourself permission to make mistakes with your new thinking, and use any setbacks as opportunities to discover more about your beliefs.

Dealing with your doubts and reservations

You must give full range to your scepticism when you're changing your beliefs. If you try to sweep your doubts under the carpet, those doubts can re-emerge when you least expect it – usually when you're in a stressful situation. Consider Sylvester's experience:

> Sylvester, or Sly for short, believes that other people must like him and goes out of his way to put people at ease in social situations. Sly takes great care to never hurt anyone's feelings and puts pressure on himself to be a good host. Not surprisingly, Sly's often worn out by his efforts. Because Sly's work involves managing other staff, he also feels anxious much of the time. Sly also worries about confrontation and what his staff members think of him when he disciplines them.
>
> After having some CBT, Sly concludes that his beliefs need to change if he's ever going to overcome his anxiety and feelings of panic at work. Sly formulates a healthy alternative belief: 'I want to be liked by others, but I don't always *have* to be liked. Being disliked is tolerable and doesn't mean I'm an unlikeable person.'
>
> Sly can see how this new belief makes good sense and can help him feel less anxious about confronting staff members or being not-so-super-entertaining in social situations. But deep inside, Sly feels stirrings of doubt. Still, Sly denies his reservations about the new belief and ignores niggling uncertainty. One day, when Sly's confronting a staff member about persistent lateness, his underlying doubts rear up. Sly resorts to his old belief because he hasn't dealt with his doubts effectively. Sly ends up letting his worker off the hook and feeling angry with himself for not dealing with the matter properly.

Had Sly faced up to his misgivings about allowing himself to be disliked, he may have given himself a chance to resolve his feeling. Sly may then have been more prepared to deal with the stressful situation without resorting to his old belief and avoidant behaviour.

Zigging and zagging through the zigzag technique

Use the zigzag technique to strengthen your belief in a new, healthy alternative belief or attitude. The zigzag technique involves playing devil's advocate with yourself. The more you argue the case in favour of a healthy belief and challenge your own attacks on it, the more deeply you can come to believe in it. Figure 12-1 shows a completed zigzag form based on Sly's example.

To go through the zigzag technique, do the following steps:

1. **Write down in the top left-hand box of the zigzag form a belief that you want to strengthen.**

   On the form, rate how strongly you endorse this belief, from 0 to 100 per cent conviction.

   Be sure that the belief's consistent with reality or true, logical and helpful to you. See the 'Generating arguments to support your helpful alternative belief' section earlier in this chapter for more on testing your healthy belief.

2. **In the next box down, write your doubts, reservations or challenges about the healthy belief.**

   Really let yourself attack the belief, using all the unhealthy arguments that come to mind.

3. **In the next box, dispute your attack and redefend the healthy belief.**

   Focus on defending the healthy belief. Don't become sidetracked by any points raised in your attack from Step 2.

4. **Repeat Steps 2 and 3 until you exhaust all your attacks on the healthy belief.**

   Be sure to use up all your doubts and reservations about choosing to really go for the new, healthy alternative way of thinking. Use as many forms as you need and be sure to stop on a defence of the belief you want to establish rather than on an attack.

5. **Re-rate, from 0 to 100 per cent, how strongly you endorse the healthy belief after going through all your doubts.**

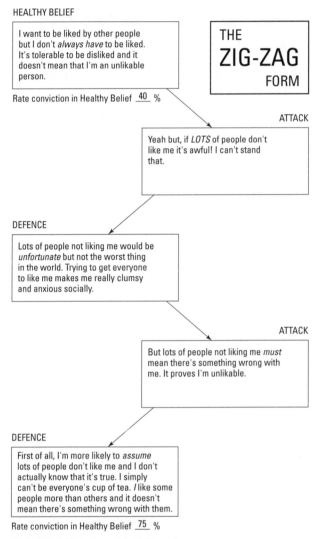

HEALTHY BELIEF

I want to be liked by other people but I don't *always have* to be liked. It's tolerable to be disliked and it doesn't mean that I'm an unlikable person.

THE
ZIG-ZAG
FORM

Rate conviction in Healthy Belief _40_ %

ATTACK

Yeah but, if *LOTS* of people don't like me it's awful! I can't stand that.

DEFENCE

Lots of people not liking me would be *unfortunate* but not the worst thing in the world. Trying to get everyone to like me makes me really clumsy and anxious socially.

ATTACK

But lots of people not liking me *must* mean there's something wrong with me. It proves I'm unlikable.

DEFENCE

First of all, I'm more likely to *assume* lots of people don't like me and I don't actually know that it's true. I simply can't be everyone's cup of tea. *I* like some people more than others and it doesn't mean there's something wrong with them.

Rate conviction in Healthy Belief _75_ %

Figure 12-1: Sly's completed zigzag form.

If your conviction in the healthy belief hasn't increased or has increased only slightly, revisit the previous instructions on how to use the zigzag form. Or, if you have a CBT therapist, discuss the form with her and see whether she can spot where you zigged when you should have zagged.

Putting your new beliefs to the test

Doing pen-and-paper exercises is great – they really can help you to move your new beliefs from your head to your heart.

However, the best way to make your new ways of thinking more automatic is to put them to the test. Putting them to the test means going into familiar situations where your old attitudes are typically triggered, and acting according to your new way of thinking.

So, our friend Sly from earlier in the chapter may choose to do the following to test his new beliefs:

✔ Sly confronts his member of staff about her lateness in a forthright manner. Sly bears the discomfort of upsetting her and remembers that being disliked by one worker doesn't prove that he's an unlikeable person.

✔ Sly throws a party and resists the urge to make himself busy entertaining everyone and playing the host.

✔ Sly works less hard in work and social situations at putting everyone at ease and trying to be super-likeable mister nice guy.

If you're really, really serious about making your new beliefs stick, you can *seek out* situations in which to test them. On top of using your new beliefs and their knock-on new behaviours in everyday situations, try setting difficult tests for yourself. Sit down and think about it: if you were still operating under your old beliefs, what situations would really freak you out? Go there. Doing so will 'up the ante' with regard to endorsing your new beliefs.

Coping with everyday situations, such as Sly's previous example, are very useful, and they're often enough to move your new belief from your head to your heart. But if you really want to put your new beliefs under strain, with a view to making them even stronger, put yourself into out-of-the-ordinary situations. For example, try deliberately doing something ridiculous in public or being purposefully rude and aloof. See if you can remain resolute in your new belief such as 'disapproval does not mean unworthiness' in the face of your most feared outcomes. We think you can! This is a tried and tested CBT tool for overcoming all sorts of problems, such as social anxiety.

Here are some tests that Sly (or we could now call him 'Braveheart') may set up for himself:

- ✔ Go into shops and deliberately be impolite by not saying 'thank you' and not smiling at the shop assistant. This test requires Sly to bear the discomfort of possibly leaving the shop assistant unhappy after making a poor impression.

- ✔ Say good morning to staff without smiling and allow them to form the impression that he's 'in a bad mood'.

- ✔ Mooch about, deliberately trying to look moody and aloof in a social setting.

- ✔ Make a complaint about faulty goods he's purchased from a local shop where the staff know him.

- ✔ Bump into someone on public transport and don't apologise.

You may think that Sly's setting himself up to be utterly friendless as a result of this wretched belief change lark. On the contrary. Sly has friends. Sly still has a reputation of being a generally kind and affable bloke. What Sly doesn't have now is a debilitating belief that he has to please all the people all the time. Rather, Sly can come to truly believe that he can tolerate the discomfort of upsetting people occasionally and that being disliked by one or more people is part of being human. That's life. That's the way it goes sometimes. Sly can believe in his heart that he's a fallible human, just like everyone else, that he's capable of being liked and disliked, but basically he's okay.

Nurturing Your New Beliefs

As you continue to live with your alternative helpful beliefs, gather evidence that supports your new beliefs. Becoming more aware of evidence from yourself, other people and the world around you that supports your new, more helpful way of thinking, is one of the keys to strengthening your beliefs and keeping them strong.

A *positive data log* is a record of evidence you collect that shows the benefits of holding your new belief. The positive data log helps you overcome the biased, prejudiced way in which you keep unhelpful beliefs well-fed, by soaking up evidence that fits with them and discounting or distorting evidence that doesn't fit. Using a positive data log boosts the available data that fit your new belief and helps you to retrain yourself to take in the positive.

Your positive data log is simply a record of positive results arising from acting in accordance with a healthy new belief and evidence that contradicts your old, unhealthy belief. You can use any type of notebook to record your evidence. Follow these steps:

1. **Write your new belief at the top of a page.**

2. **Record evidence that your new belief is helpful to you; include changes in your emotions and behaviour.**

3. **Record positive reactions that you get from others when you act in accordance with new beliefs.**

4. **Record any experiences that contradict your old belief.**

   Be specific and include even the smallest details that encourage you to doubt your old way of thinking. For example, even a newspaper vendor making small talk when you buy your paper can be used as evidence against a belief that you're unlikeable.

5. **Make sure that you record every bit of information in support of your new belief and in contradiction to your old belief.**

   Fill up the whole notebook if you can.

If you still have trouble believing that an old, unhelpful belief is true, start by collecting evidence on a daily basis that your old belief isn't 100 per cent true, 100 per cent of the time. Collecting this sort of evidence can help you steadily erode how true the belief seems.

In your positive data log, you can list the benefits of operating under your new belief, including all the ways in which your fears about doing so have been disproved.

For example, Sly might record the following observations:

- ✔ His staff members still seem to generally like being managed by him, despite the fact that he disciplines them when needed.

- ✔ Being less gregarious at parties doesn't stop others from having a good time or from engaging with him.

- ✔ His anxiety and panic about the possibility of being disliked have reduced in response to his belief change.

Your positive data log can not only remind you of the good results you've reaped from changing your unhealthy beliefs to healthy ones, but also help you be *compassionate* with yourself when you relapse to your unhealthy beliefs and corresponding behaviours. Use your positive data log to chart your progress, so when you *do* fall back you can assure yourself that your setback need be only temporary. After all, practice makes imperfect.

Many people add to their positive data log for months or even years. Keeping the log provides them with a useful antidote to the natural tendency to be overly self-critical.

Be sure to refer to your positive data log often, even daily, or several times each day when you're bedding down new beliefs. Keep it in your desk or handbag or wherever you're most likely to be able to access it during the day. As a general rule, you can't look at your positive data log too often!

Chapter 13

Heading for a Healthier and Happier Life

In This Chapter

▶ Discovering and choosing healthy activities

▶ Taking care of yourself, your life and your relationships

▶ Communicating effectively

▶ Evaluating and adhering to your values

*T*he way that you think influences the way that you feel and behave. How you behave also influences the way you end up feeling and thinking . . . and round and round the cycle goes.

So, how you *live* from day to day has an effect on your overall mood. In this chapter, we look at what makes a lifestyle *healthy*. Developing a healthy lifestyle can contribute enormously to keeping you in tip-top physical and psychological condition.

We use the term 'healthy' to mean looking after your physical self, which includes exercise, sleep, sex, your eating habits, and keeping your living environment a pleasant place to be. Psychological health is about doing things that give you a sense of enjoyment and achievement, holding helpful and balanced attitudes toward life, and building satisfying relationships.

Being in tip-top psychological and emotional health also involves revisiting your values. Taking a thorough look at what is *really* most important to you, and making time in your busy schedule to reflect your values through regular action, greatly contributes to an overall sense of well-being.

Make looking after yourself a priority rather than an after-thought. An ounce of prevention really is worth a pound of cure.

Planning to Prevent Relapse

Once you start to recover from your problems, your next step is to devise a plan to prevent a resurgence of symptoms – to ensure that you don't suffer a *relapse*. A relapse basically means that you return to your original state of mind. An important part of your relapse prevention plan is nurturing yourself and guarding against falling back into old, unhelpful lifestyle habits, such as working too late, eating unhealthily, drinking too much caffeine and alcohol, or isolating yourself. Chapter 15 deals with relapse prevention in depth. The following sections in this chapter provide some pointers on how you can make your life fuller and how to take better care of yourself.

Filling In the Gaps

When you start to recover from some types of emotional problem, such as depression, anxiety or obsessions, you may find that you have a considerable amount of spare time available to you, which previously your symptoms took up. Indeed, you may be astounded to find out just how much energy, attention and time common psychological difficulties can actually consume.

Finding constructive and enjoyable things to do to fill in the gaps where your symptoms once were is important. Keeping yourself occupied with pursuits that are meaningful to you (and reflect your core values and priorities) gives you a sense of well-being and leaves less opportunity for your symptoms to re-emerge.

Choosing absorbing activities

Activities that you used to enjoy may take a back seat while you wrestle with your problems. However, maybe you can think of some new activities that interest you and that you may like to try. The following are a few pointers to help you generate ideas about what activities and hobbies you can begin building into your life:

- ✔ Make a list of things you used to do and would like to start doing again.

- ✔ Make a separate list of new activities that you'd like to try.

- ✔ Try to create a balance between activities that do and don't involve physical exercise.

- ✔ Include everyday activities like cooking, reading, DIY and keeping up social contacts. These activities are often neglected when you're overwhelmed by symptoms.

- ✔ Choose to focus on around five activities to revive or pursue, depending on how full your life is with work and family commitments.

In case you're still at a loss as to what you want to do, here's some ideas – but remember that this list is by no means exhaustive: antiques, art appreciation, astronomy, baking, chess, dance, drama, dressmaking, enamelling, fishing, football, gardening, golf, interior decorating, kick boxing, languages, motoring, painting, pets Rhena has a cat called Jack, who's transformed her life! And since the first publication of this book she's also acquired a West Highland terrier called Powder Puff, who's the most adorable and consuming creature . . . everyone agrees . . . possibly even Jack), quizzes, tennis, voluntary work, wine-tasting, writing . . .

Pets are great companions. But they also require some considerable work and commitment (especially dogs, no matter how small). Before you decide to get a pet, do some research to determine the best pet for your living environment, work routine and financial situation. Otherwise you may find yourself lumbered with an animal that's far more high maintenance than you initially expected.

Don't just think about it! Decide *when* you're going to begin doing your chosen activities. If you don't give yourself a concrete start date, forgetting about things or putting them off can be all too easy.

Matchmaking your pursuits

You know yourself better than anyone else, so you're the best person to judge which hobbies can bring you the most satisfaction. Try to match your recreational pursuits to your character. If you know that you love paying attention to detail, you may enjoy needlework or making jewellery. Extreme sports may appeal to you if you've always been good at physical activities and like adrenalin rushes. Conversely, if you've never been very musical, taking up an instrument may not be the best choice for you.

We recommend that you stretch yourself by trying things that you haven't done before. Who knows – you may end up really liking the new activities. However, if you choose pursuits that are too far removed from your fundamental personality or natural abilities, you might lose heart and abandon them.

Putting personal pampering into practice

Oh, the joys of a good massage, a hot foamy bath or a trip to the opera (okay, we understand that not everyone feels the same about opera). You can't overcome your problems without a significant degree of personal effort. Congratulate yourself for your hard work, and treat yourself to a few nice things.

Take care of yourself on a day-to-day basis, and look out for times when you deserve a few extra special treats. Friday nights are a good time to regularly treat yourself after a long week at work.

Your treats don't have to be expensive. You can do many small things – such as putting some cut flowers in a vase, making your living space smell nice, playing pleasant music, watching a favourite film or television programme – which are free or inexpensive.

Consider pampering yourself as part of your *relapse-prevention plan* (see Chapter 15 for more on relapse prevention). Even doing little things like using nice bath oils or eating a special meal once a week can remind you to value yourself and to treat yourself with loving care.

Overhauling Your Lifestyle

We suggest that you take a close look at the way you currently live and decide on the things that are good and the things that are not so good for you. Be sure to consider the following key areas:

- ✔ **Regular and healthy eating.** The principle is relatively simple: have three meals and a couple of healthy snacks a day, with plenty of fruit, vegetables and wholegrain foods. Minimise your consumption of sugar and simple carbohydrates, like white bread, and don't overdo the saturated fat. Have what you fancy in moderation. If you think you need extra help with healthy eating, talk to your doctor, who can refer you to a dietician.

  Try keeping a record of everything you eat, for a week. Identify where you can make positive changes towards eating more regularly and more healthily. If you find that your actions don't match with your good intentions, tackle the thoughts and attitudes that can get in the way of healthy eating.

- ✔ **Regular exercise.** Ample evidence suggests that exercise is very beneficial for both your mental and physical health. Aim for at least three sessions of physical exercise, lasting 20–30 minutes each, per week (five sessions is ideal, but you may need to build up to it). Consult your doctor if you haven't exercised regularly for some time.

- ✔ **Leisure pursuits.** Include activities that bring you pleasure or satisfaction and aren't attached to your job or home life. Remind yourself of what you used to do and of what you've been meaning to do, when choosing activities and hobbies.

- ✔ **Social contact.** Get to know new people or reinvigorate your existing relationships. Sometimes relationships suffer as a result of psychological illness. See the 'Getting intimate' section later in this chapter which talks about intimacy and communication.

- ✔ **Vitally-absorbing interests.** Get involved with causes you feel are important, such as recycling or animal rights campaigns. Even small, everyday actions like smiling at a shopkeeper, holding the door for a stranger, forgiving an indiscretion or picking up a bit of litter can help you recognise that you're contributing to the kind of world you'd like to live in.

✔ **Resource management.** This catch-all may involve you drawing up a budget, getting an accountant, developing a system to deal with your household bills efficiently, rene-gotiating your working hours, earmarking time for relaxation, arranging some babysitting or hiring a cleaner.

Ideally, you can create a nice balance between the different aspects of your life so that none is neglected.

Everyone needs delineated time for the replenishment of psychological and physical energy *as well* as for getting things done. Be aware of both – because you can't have one without the other.

Look at the things you do on a daily or weekly basis, and decide what you're doing *too much of*, such as drinking in the pub, working late or eating fast food. Try to replace some of these activities with others that you're doing too little of, such as getting exercise, spending time with your family, cooking tasty, healthy meals or studying.

Walking the walk

The best-laid plans of mice and men are apt to go astray. And how.

You're really serious about making positive changes to your lifestyle; however, just thinking about it and setting out plans aren't enough – although they *are* a great first step. The next step is to *do it*! Actions speak louder than words, so act on your intentions sooner rather than later.

Keeping your body moving

We cannot emphasise enough the multiple benefits of you taking regular exercise. It's so good for you, in so many ways. If you don't believe us, try it out! Exercise a few times each week and see if you don't end up feeling better – we defy you to contradict us.

You can exercise in ways that don't involve going to the gym. Gardening, walking, cycling, dancing and housework all give your body a workout. Find out which activities suit your interests, schedule and current level of fitness – *and do them!*

Be careful that you're exercising for the right reasons, such as to enjoy yourself, de-stress and keep physically and mentally healthy. Check that you're not exercising obsessively. The following are unhealthy motivations for taking exercise:

✔ **To keep your weight lower than is medically recommended.** People who suffer from eating disorders often exercise fanatically.

✔ **To improve your looks.** People with body dysmorphic disorder (BDD) sometimes use exercise to compensate for imagined defects in their physical appearance Also, if you have a very poor body image or an eating disorder, you may exercise in an attempt to make yourself more physically acceptable to yourself and others.

✔ **To punish yourself.** People with feelings of shame and low self-worth may exercise to excess as a means of self-harming.

Ask your physician to work out your *body mass index* or 'BMI', which gives you a weight range that is normal for your age and height.

Using your head

Perhaps your emotional problems get in the way of your work or study. Maybe your difficulties interfere with you making progress in your career or changing jobs – after all, many people with psychological problems also experience work and education difficulties.

Start to set goals for how you'd like your work or academic life to develop. Build a realistic plan of action for reaching your professional or educational goals by following these steps:

1. **Start your plan by considering where you'd like to be and what you need to do in terms of study and training to get there.**

2. **Break your ultimate goal down into smaller, bite-sized chunks.** You may need to gather references, build a portfolio, write a CV or apply for a loan or grant to fund your studies.

3. **Investigate facilities for learning.** Use the Internet to look for specific courses, contact universities and colleges for a prospectus, see a careers advisor or visit an employment agency.

4. **Build your study or training plan into your life with a view to keeping a balance between study, work, social and leisure activities.**

5. **Set a realistic timeframe to achieve your goal.** Pushing yourself to get there too fast is likely to cause you stress, impair your enjoyment of the journey to your goal, or even lead you to abandon your goal all together.

Go out and study just for the sake of it. Developing a new skill or exploring a new subject area can be highly rewarding for you, whether or not the studying is applicable directly to your work. Adult education classes and intensive workshops can be a great way for you to explore new topics – and for you to meet new people, which can be beneficial if your social life has suffered during your illness.

Getting involved

Think about the kind of world you want to live in and how you can contribute towards creating it. You can get involved with anti-litter campaigns, local building-restoration projects, charities, or whatever you feel is important. You can usually choose how much time to devote to these pursuits.

Becoming spiritual

Sometimes people with specific disorders, such as obsessive-compulsive disorder (OCD) or extreme guilt, can find that their religion or spiritual beliefs get mixed up with their problems. Re-establishing a healthy understanding of your faith can be an important aspect of your recovery. Resuming your usual manner of worship – be it meditation, attending mass or going to a synagogue – can help you to reintegrate with your religious beliefs or your community. You might also find that discussing your recent problems with a religious leader or a member of your congregation is helpful.

Talking the talk

Emotional problems can have a detrimental effect on your personal relationships. Sometimes, your symptoms can be so all-consuming that you have little space to show interest in what others around you are feeling and doing. Therefore, you may need to do some work to rebuild your existing relationships when you feel better.

Six steps for talking and listening

Good relationships are sustained by thoughtfulness, effort and time. Many of the changes in your relationships may occur naturally because as you become less preoccupied with your problems you're more able to focus on the world around you.

Effective communication is the cornerstone of good relationships. Bear in mind that you can communicate not only with what you say, but also with how you *listen*. Your body language can also convey a message to others. Things like eye contact and physical contact are also means of getting the message across. A simple hug can really mean a lot.

Try the following six steps to improve your communication skills:

1 When you have something important to discuss with someone, find a mutually good time to do so. Make sure that you both have ample time to talk and listen to each other.

2 Use 'I feel' statements, such as '*I feel* disappointed that you came home late', rather than blaming language, such as '*You* made me so angry'.

3 If you want to give negative feedback to someone about his behaviour, keep it clear, brief and specific. Remember to also give positive feedback about the behaviour you want to reinforce, for example thank your partner for calling to say he'll be late.

4 After you've given positive or negative feedback, ask the person how he feels and what he thinks about what you've said.

5 Don't fall into the trap of thinking that a right or true way of doing things exists. Accept that different people value different things. Seek compromises when appropriate. Listen to the other person's point of view.

6 Be prepared to accept negative feedback and criticism from others. Look for points that you agree with in what the other person is saying. Give the other person a chance to air his views before you get defensive or counteractive. Give yourself time to assess the feedback you receive.

When your symptoms subside, you may want to give more of your attention to the other people in your life. This may involve playing with your kids, talking to your partner about how your problems have affected your relationship (without blaming yourself, of course) or renewing contact with friends and extended family.

People in your life are likely to be aware of how troubled you've been and they may notice recent positive changes in you. Let them talk about the changes they've noticed within you. Listening to other people's experiences of your problems can help to reinforce the idea that the other people in your life care about you. Improving your relationships and simply spending time in the company of other people can help you keep your symptoms at bay. You can also involve others in your relapse-prevention plan, if appropriate.

A supportive relationship with a significant other can help you to stay healthy. This relationship doesn't need to be a romantic one – platonic relationships are important as well. Research has shown that having a network of social contacts, as well as having someone you're able to confide in, helps to reduce your emotional problems in general.

It's never too late for you to make friends. Even if your problems have led you to isolate yourself, now's the time to go out and meet people. Be patient and give yourself the time and opportunity to start forming good relationships. Go to where the people are! Join some clubs or classes.

Getting intimate

Your specific problems may lead you to avoid intimate relationships with other people. You may have been too preoccupied by your problems to be able to form or maintain intimate relationships. If you want to be close to others, you've got to get your head round the concept of letting others into your life. Allowing yourself to trust others enough to share at least some of your personal history can make you feel closer to your listeners. Intimacy is a give-and-take affair – ideally, the balance is roughly equal.

If you think you're incapable of getting truly close to someone else, you're probably wrong. Give other people – and yourself – a chance to be honest with each other. Reciprocally-enhancing relationships usually evolve naturally, but you need to be open to the possibilities of intimate relationships for this evolution to happen.

Sex and other animals

Your interest in sex, regardless of your age or gender, may diminish as a result of your emotional disturbance. Many people dealing with emotional problems can lose interest in sex. When you begin to feel better, getting your sex life back on track may take some time.

Sex drive is a bit like appetite: you don't always realise you're hungry until you start eating.

Sometimes, couples stop having sex regularly but don't ever discuss the change. Often, both partners get into a routine of not being sexually intimate and try to ignore the problem. Some people are too shy to talk about sex or feel guilty for having lost interest in it. Additionally, many people are too embarrassed to discuss their loss of sex drive with their doctor, or indeed friends.

Taking the plunge and talking about changes in your sex drive with your therapist or doctor can be very worthwhile. Your therapist or doctor may offer you useful suggestions and may even tell you that certain medications you've been taking may contribute to your decreased interest in sex.

Loss of interest in sexual activities is a normal side effect of certain experiences. Many psychological disorders, such as depression, post-traumatic stress disorder, obsessional problems, health anxiety, postnatal depression and low self-esteem, can impact your ability to feel aroused. Bereavement, physical illness and stress can also put your sexual desires on the backburner. Fortunately, decreased libido is often temporary.

Talking about sex

'Birds do it, bees do it, even educated fleas do it', but sometimes the issue of sex is like an elephant in a tutu doing the dance of the seven veils in the middle of your bedroom. Both you and your partner can end up studiously ignoring its presence, even though it's right there, begging for your attention.

If you can't bring yourself to broach the topic of sex with your partner as you begin to recover, you can do a few things to help rekindle the flames of desire. Try some of the following:

- **Resume non-sexual physical contact.** Hold hands, stroke your partner's arm or back as you chat, sit closer to each other on the sofa and reintroduce cuddling. Non-sexual contact can help you to get comfortable with touching one another again, and set the scene for a revival of more intimate contact.

- **Kiss.** If you've got into the habit of a quick kiss on the cheek as you leave the house, aim for the mouth instead. Kissing is a powerful form of communication. It also can be highly sensual and enjoyable.

- **Create opportunities.** Getting into bed at the same time, before you're both bone tired, and then snuggling up can create a non-threatening reintroduction to sexual relations.

- **Take the pressure off.** If you tell yourself that you've *got* to get aroused or you've *got* to have sex tonight, you can work yourself into such a state that all spontaneity is quashed. Try to take the attitude that if it happens, it happens.

- **Give yourself a chance to get in the mood.** You don't have to feel very aroused to start getting intimate. Sometimes you may need to have a lot of low-level sexual contact like stroking petting, and kissing before you're ready to go further. Be patient with yourself and try to talk to your partner about how you're feeling. Sometimes, just talking about sex is enough to relax you to let nature take its course.

- **Take the onus off orgasm.** Any sexual or close physical contact can be fulfilling. You may not be able to achieve orgasm for some time, so instead enjoy foreplay like you may have done in the early stages of your relationship. For example, kissing is a very powerful form of expression. You can really get your sex life back on track, and you may even be able to make it better than it was before, if you give a lot of attention to the preliminaries.

Whatever turns you on is worth exploring further. Talk to your partner: you may be able to find things that can help you both get more in the mood for lovemaking. Try to be open-minded about your sex life. Just be careful to set your own personal boundaries about what turns you on and what has the opposite effect.

Living in Line with Your Values

Most people enjoy life most when they consistently act in accordance with their personal values. People we see in CBT treatment typically report better mood, improved self-opinion, a general sense of well-being and of 'being true to themselves' – once they've identified and started to act in line with their individual value systems.

By 'values' we mean the things in life that are most important to you: your personal ethics, morals, philosophies, ideals, standards and principles. Sometimes, however, your depression, anxiety, poor self-esteem and other types of emotional problem can relegate your interests and values to the sidelines. Now is the time to rediscover and honour them, in the interest of your continued mental health and happiness.

Because all people are unique individuals, you won't always share the same values. That said, however, people with similar values are generally attracted to one another and end up in the same places. You may find like-minded people at workshops, rallies, charitable events, courses, and so on. So taking a closer look at your personal values can potentially have the additional benefit of enriching your social life.

 Getting back in touch with your core values can be difficult if your mind has been clouded with anxieties and dark thoughts for some time. Be patient with yourself and permit yourself time to rediscover what you're all about.

Use the items in this list to help you pinpoint your personal principles:

- ✔ Work and career
- ✔ Study and skills-based training
- ✔ Community involvement
- ✔ Neighbourhood watch projects
- ✔ Cultural pursuits and identity

- ✔ Religion and spirituality
- ✔ Sports and other active hobbies
- ✔ Nature, animal welfare, wildlife and the environment
- ✔ Friendships and friendship groups (book clubs, social clubs and so on)
- ✔ Family and home life
- ✔ Causes and charities
- ✔ Politics
- ✔ Travel
- ✔ Overall social responsibility
- ✔ Art, music and theatre (either observing or participating)
- ✔ Reading for pleasure
- ✔ Cooking
- ✔ Doing crafts like woodwork, knitting or pottery
- ✔ Upholding standards for social conduct, such as being polite, friendly and assisting others

This list merely outlines some of the more common areas of value-based activity. Don't be restricted by it! Be creative – think both big and small. Anything you do in honour of your values, minor or major, is equally valid and beneficial (to you and those around you).

For example, one of our colleagues has a strict rule of conduct that she leaves a public toilet in the state she'd like to find it (an often grim task!). Another mutual friend values the services of his local rubbish collectors very highly. He habitually thanks them heartily and always tips them when appropriate.

You may find defining your personal values easier if you reflect on the values of a person you respect and admire. Try following these steps:

1. **Think of someone that you either know very well (like a friend or family member) or you know a lot about (maybe a celebrity or historical figure). Record their name on a sheet of paper.**

2. **Make a list of the values they seem to hold, have openly talked about or demonstrate through their**

actions. Chances are that you'll realise that you
share some basic values with this person.

3. **Make specific notes about the things your admired
person does that support and reflect their personal
(and your shared) values.**

4. **Make definite plans to follow this person's example!**
Write down things you can do and when you can
realistically do them. Use the blank form in Figure
13-2, later in this chapter to help you organise your
thoughts. Don't forget the tiny, everyday things that
can really have a positive impact on yourself and
others.

The purpose of this experiment is to help you remember
and recognise what's most important to *you*. Nobody has a
monopoly on values, so sharing them is a natural and normal
part of life. Just beware of unwittingly adopting other people's
values because self-doubt tells you that your own views and
opinions can't be trusted. Allow others to provide you with
inspiration but make up your own mind about your values.

Reflecting your values through action

Identifying your values can be easier said than done. But you
can help yourself become more value aware by asking yourself some basic questions. Consider the following example.

Callum has battled with social anxiety for the past five years
(for more on this, see Chapter 8). Though always a sensitive
and shy child, Callum's anxiety about what others may think
of him came to a head during late adolescence. Adolescence
is a common time for people to develop social anxiety. Callum
has spent so many years worrying, striving to impress his
peers, guessing and trying to influence other people's opinions of him that he's largely forgotten what he *actually* thinks
about things *himself*.

Like many people struggling with poor self-esteem and
extreme fear of being judged negatively by others, Callum
consistently held beliefs like 'others know better than me' and
'my opinions don't carry much weight'. As a result of this way
of thinking, Callum's values, interests and opinions have been

seriously neglected. Happily, he successfully used CBT to get himself out of the trap of social anxiety.

Here are some of the questions Callum asked himself to help get reacquainted with his forgotten values, opinions and interests:

✔ What were my earlier interests before social anxiety overtook my thinking?

> *I used to be interested in mechanics and vintage cars. I also used to really enjoy sci-fi films and novels. I still have an interest in these two areas today.*

✔ If I put the opinions of others to one side, what might be some of my personal principles and mottos?

> *I believe in living in a socially responsible manner that adds to the community around me.*

> *I believe in 'working to live' rather than 'living to work'.*

> *I believe in supporting the rights of less privileged, vulnerable groups such as the elderly, people with disabilities, those living in poverty and animals.*

✔ What pursuits do I get really passionate about?

> *Supporting charities that aim to improve the lives of children and the elderly.*

> *Being a responsible pet owner.*

> *Supporting sustainable farming and reducing CO_2 emissions. Travelling and enjoying nature. Reading and learning for pleasure.*

> *Being consistently polite and friendly to other people.*

Whether social anxiety, general poor self-esteem, depression or some other problem has over-shadowed your values, you can apply the same questions Callum used to yourself.

Once you've made yourself familiar with your core values, honouring them through deliberate and persistent action makes sense. Doing so is very likely to improve your overall enjoyment and give you a sense of living your life well. In order to turn your good intentions into actions, make a plan.

Callum made some plans to live more consistently with his values. He identified several actions that reflect his principles and interests and scheduled in clear times for carrying them out, as shown in Table 13-1.

Table 13-1   Callum's value-based behaviours form.

Value	Related Activity	Frequency
Working to live	Booking regular time off	Booking holiday times at the start of each year
Responsible pet ownership	Taking my dog for a long walk	Thrice weekly
Supporting vulnerable groups	Donating to charities	Monthly
Reducing CO_2 emissions	Walking to work	Daily
Being polite to others	Saying 'thank you', smiling at those I meet	Daily
Reading and learning for pleasure	Reading novels	Twice weekly

Use the blank form provided in Table 13-2 to schedule in your own value-based behaviours.

Table 13-2   My value-based behaviours form.

Value	Related Activity	Frequency

Wanting to be accepted and feel part of a larger social group is human nature. However, bear in mind that, whilst the thoughts and views of people around you are important, they aren't more important than your own. Nor is it necessary to base your self-image solely on the way others seem to think about you. You can reject other people's judgements of you entirely or in part, or accept them if you think they're accurate. At the end of the day, you know yourself better than anyone else does.

Staying focused on what's most important

Unearthing your basic broad values can help you to remember what things in your life are most important to you on a day-to-day basis. Sometimes the pressures of modern living can skew your idea of what matters. For example, being at a work meeting may seem more important than attending your nephew's school play. However later, when he's excitedly telling you how he remembered all his lines, you may regret having put work demands first.

You can't always do what's fundamentally most important to you without incurring unwanted consequences, of course. However, if you scrutinise things more closely, you'll probably find several opportunities to honour the important things in life rather than blindly responding to external pressures from work, and so on.

Reshuffling priorities

Knowing your personal values really well also helps you to prioritise daily duties more effectively. In general, your priorities will be compatible with and mirror your intrinsic value system.

Review your work in the previous sections of this chapter and make a numbered list of your personal priorities. Keep your list handy and refer to it regularly as a reminder of how you ideally want to live your life.

Priorities shift and shuffle according to what's actually going on in your life. For example, putting work first (for a time) if you need extra money to pay off debts is normal and constructive. Or you may carve out extra time for your elderly relative during his convalescence from an operation. Remind yourself, however, that changes in your fundamental priorities are usually temporary; reshuffle them once a crisis has passed.

Chapter 14

Overcoming Obstacles to Progress

. . . .

In This Chapter

▶ Getting to know the feelings that bind you

▶ Taking a progressive attitude

▶ Avoiding getting stuck on the road to recovery

. . . .

*H*uman beings have a keen way of blocking their progress and sabotaging their goals. Maybe you obstruct your progress without even being aware that you're doing it. Or perhaps you're conscious that you're sabotaging yourself with faulty thinking. Whatever the case, this chapter explores common obstacles that get in the way of positive change, and suggests some tips for overcoming blocks to progress.

Tackling Emotions That Get in the Way of Change

As if having an emotional problem isn't enough, you may be giving yourself an extra helping of discomfort and distress as a result of some of the meanings you attach to your original problems. Some of the feelings that you may experience about your primary emotional problems, such as shame, guilt or even pride, can result in *progress paralysis*.

Shifting shame

When people feel ashamed of their problems, they usually believe that their symptoms are a sign that they're weak, flawed or defective. If you feel ashamed, you're less likely to seek help, because you worry that other people may judge you harshly for having a psychological problem, such as depression, or perhaps they may think that you're silly for having other types of problems, such as anxiety. You may worry that anyone you tell about your problem will be horrified by some of your thoughts or actions, and reject you. You may be too ashamed to even admit to yourself that you have a problem. Blaming the problem on external events or other people is often a result of shame. Shame is really corrosive to change because it can:

- ✔ Make you isolate yourself, which can lower your mood even further.

- ✔ Lead you to deny the problem. And you can't work on problem-solving if you're unwilling to acknowledge that the problem exists in the first place.

- ✔ Result in you blaming other people and events for your problems, robbing you of your personal power for change.

- ✔ Make you overestimate your symptoms as 'abnormal', 'weird' or 'unacceptable'.

- ✔ Lead you to overestimate the harsh degree by which others judge you for having the problem.

- ✔ Stop you from seeking out more information that can help to make you realise that your problem isn't so unusual.

- ✔ Prevent you from getting appropriate psychological help, or the right medication.

Fight back against shame by refusing to hide your problems from yourself. Seek out information to make some of your experiences seem more normal. Practise self-acceptance beliefs like the ones we outline in Chapter 10. Take responsibility for overcoming your emotional problems – but resist blaming yourself for your symptoms.

Getting rid of guilt

Guilt is an unhealthy negative emotion that's particularly notorious for blocking positive change. You may be telling yourself guilt-provoking things like the following:

- ✔ 'I'm causing my family a lot of bother through my problems.'

- ✔ 'Other people in the world are so much worse off than me. I've no right to feel depressed.'

- ✔ 'I should be more productive. Instead, I'm just a waste of space.'

Guilt sabotages your chances of taking positive action. Guilty thoughts, such as the preceding examples, can lead you to put yourself down further, thereby making yourself more depressed. Your depression leads you to see the future as hopeless and saps your motivation. (Have a peek at Chapter 5 for more information about unhealthy negative emotions and how they work against you.)

Even if the thoughts that are making you feel guilty about your depression, anxiety or other emotional problem hold some truth, try to accept yourself as someone who's *unwell*. For example, your diminished ability to be productive is a side effect of depression, not an indication that you're a bad or selfish person.

Shame and guilt grow in the dark. Hiding your problems, and your feelings *about* your problems, from other people tends to make things worse over time. Talking about your depression or other problems gives you the chance to share your fears and discomfort with someone else, who may be far more understanding than you imagine.

Putting aside pride

Having too much pride can get in the way of your progress. Sometimes, pride is a sort of compensatory strategy for feelings of shame. Your pride may protect you from the shame that you think you'd experience if you were to accept that the methods you've used thus far to overcome your problems have been less than ideal. The following are common pride-based attitudes that may be stopping you from making positive changes:

✔ **'It's absurd to say that I can help myself – if I could make myself better, I'd have done it ages ago!'** Actually, people very rarely know how best to help themselves out of emotional problems. Often, you need to read some self-help books or have techniques explained to you before you really understand how to implement specific techniques, and why these methods work.

✔ **'I'm an intelligent person and I should be able to work out this stuff on my own!'** Maybe you *can* work out how to help yourself overcome emotional problems without any help whatsoever. But remember: even the most intelligent people need to see specialists for advice from time to time. For example, you may be very bright but you still need to take your car to a mechanic to be fixed.

✔ **'I like to think of myself as strong. Admitting to having these problems shows me up as weak.'** Getting a bout of flu doesn't make you a weak person – and neither does a bout of depression or anxiety. For example, refusing to seek medical treatment for an infected wound is foolish, not an example of strength.

Swallow your pride and be ready to seek advice and help. Recognising and accepting that you have a problem and that you need to get guidance on how to deal with it, takes strength, not weakness.

Seeking support

After you begin to get over your shame, guilt and pride, you can start to look for help in earnest. The help you seek may take the form of reading a self-help book like this one, approaching a therapist, talking things over with a friend (who could even support you using this book) or looking through some online resources. Some people find that self-help techniques are enough. But if you think you need more support, be sure to get help sooner rather than later. Putting off seeking professional help when you need it only prolongs your discomfort. Don't wait until your problem has advanced to the stage where your relationships, employment situation or daily functioning are suffering before you take positive action.

Book now to avoid disappointment

Many people with emotional problems wait months or even years before sharing them with anyone else. People with depression and other anxiety problems can wait for months or years before talking about their problems with another person.

The most common reason for keeping problems under wraps is shame. Thinking that you need to keep problems a secret is quite tragic, because you end up suffering in silence needlessly. Exploring your options *now* can assure you that your symptoms are common and that you have nothing to be ashamed of. Get yourself on the road to recovery now to avoid feeling disappointed that you didn't get help sooner, and you can start to begin reclaiming enjoyment from life.

Trying a little tenderness

Shame and guilt involve kicking yourself – and really putting the boot in – when you're already feeling down. Kicking someone in an attempt to get them back on their feet just doesn't make sense.

You haven't *chosen* your problems, although you may accept that you're stuck in a pattern that's making your problems worse. Take other contributing factors into account when you think about how your problems may have started.

You can take responsibility for overcoming your emotional disturbances and you can be compassionate with yourself in the process. Being kind to yourself when you're working hard to get better makes sense, particularly if you consider that a lot of the work involves making yourself uncomfortable in the short term. Surely you deserve to give yourself a little encouragement during exposures and behavioural experiments, rather than piling on the self-criticism.

 Try being your own best friend instead of your own worst critic for a while, and see whether this helps you to make some positive strides. (Have a look at Chapter 10 for more tips on how to treat yourself with compassion.)

Adopting Positive Principles That Promote Progress

Some of the attitudes you hold probably aren't going to do you any favours as you try to overcome your emotional problems. Fortunately, you can swap your unhelpful attitudes for alternative beliefs that can give you a leg-up on the ladder to better emotional health.

Understanding that simple doesn't mean easy

Most of the steps to overcoming psychological problems with CBT are relatively simple. CBT isn't rocket science – in fact, many of the principles and recommendations may seem like common sense. However, CBT may be sense, but it ain't that common – if it was, fewer people would be suffering with emotional problems.

Even if CBT is as simple as ABC, the actual application of CBT principles is far from easy. Using CBT to help yourself requires a lot of personal *effort*, *diligence*, *repetition* and *determination*.

Because CBT seems so simple, some people get frustrated when they discover that they're not getting well fast or easily enough for their liking. If you want to make CBT work for *you*, take the attitude that getting better doesn't have to be easy. Your health is worth working for.

Being optimistic about getting better

One of the biggest blocks preventing you from getting better is refusing to believe that change is possible. Be on the look-out for negative predictions that you may be making about your ability to get better. Challenge any thoughts you have which resemble the following:

✔ 'Other people get better, but they're not as messed up as me.'

✔ 'I'll never change – I've been like this for too long.'

✔ 'This CBT stuff will never work for someone as useless as me.'

If these thoughts sound familiar, check out the 'Trying a little tenderness' section earlier in this chapter, which covers how to be a little kinder to yourself. Would you encourage a friend to believe such thoughts, or would you urge her to challenge her thinking? Try to give yourself the kind of good advice that you'd give another person with your type of problem.

Look for evidence that you *can* make changes. Remind yourself of other things you've done in the past that were difficult and required lots of effort to overcome. If you don't give a new treatment method a fair shot, then how can you possibly *know* it can't work?

 Don't fall into the trap of deciding that your problems are so special and unusual that you can't be helped by conventional methods like CBT. Sometimes, people can be quite defensive about their emotional problems because they believe that they're part of what makes them unique. You'll still be a unique person when you've recovered from your problems – you'll just be happier. Clinging to the idea that no one can possibly understand or assist you can become a self-fulfilling prophecy. You may hold rigidly to the idea of being a hopeless case because it protects you from getting your hopes up and being disappointed. Take the risk of possible disappointment for the chance of success.

Staying focused on your goals

If you want to continue making healthy progress, occasionally you need to renew your commitment to your goals. You may find that you stop dead in your tracks because you've forgotten what the point is. Or perhaps you find yourself feeling ambivalent about getting over your problems. After all, staying anxious, depressed or angry may seem easier than changing.

Remind yourself regularly of your goals and the benefits of striving to achieve these goals. You can use the cost–benefit analysis (CBA) form to reaffirm the benefits of making goal-directed changes. In Chapter 7, we describe the CBA form and give you some more information about setting goals.

Always try to set goals that are within your grasp, and you can establish shorter-term goals along the way. For example, if your goal is to move from being largely housebound to being able to travel freely, set a goal of being able to go to a particular shop to buy something specific. You can then concentrate on the steps needed to reach that particular smaller goal, before moving on to tackle larger goals.

Persevering and repeating

We often hear people say that they tried a technique or experiment once but that it didn't make them feel better. The reason for this lack of success is that once is very rarely enough. When you work at changing ingrained patterns of thinking and behaving, you're likely to have to try out new alternatives many times before you appreciate any beneficial change. You need to give yourself plenty of opportunity to get used to the new thought or behaviour. Also, you can expect new ways of thinking and behaving to feel very unnatural at first.

Think of your core beliefs and old ways of behaving as automatic responses, just like using your right hand to apply your lipstick. If you break your right arm, and are unable to use it for a while, you have to use your left hand to do so. Imagine that your new healthy beliefs and behaviours are represented by your left hand. Each time you go to use your new beliefs, they feel awkward and don't seem to work very well. Every morning when you reach for your lipstick with your broken right arm, you have to remind yourself to struggle with using your left arm instead. You find it difficult to make a good outline of your lips and on some occasions look almost clown-like. However, over time you get better and better at using your left hand to apply make-up, until one day your automatic response is to reach for the lipstick with your left hand.

People can retrain themselves into using new patterns of behaviour all the time. Think about people who are giving up smoking or changing their diets. Even moving house and altering your route to work are examples of behavioural retraining. You can retrain your thinking as well as your behaviour – perseverance and repetition apply to both.

Sidestepping sand traps

Along the path to better mental health, you're sure to encounter obstacles. The following are popular reasons for abandoning your goals or not getting started with pursuing goals in the first place:

✔ **Fearing change.** Despite feeling really miserable, you may be afraid of what'll happen if you take steps to change. You may have been depressed or anxious for so long that you can't really imagine doing anything else. Perhaps some of the people in your life are helping you to live with your problems, and you fear that by getting better you may lose those people. However, getting yourself well gives you a chance to build more fulfilling relationships and to develop your independence.

✔ **Having low-frustration tolerance.** When the going gets tough, the tough go home to bed, right? No! You may be tempted to go to bed, but you just wake up every morning with the same old problems. The only way to increase your tolerance to frustration in all its forms is to grit your teeth and stick with it. However uncomfortable you may be while working on changing yourself, the effort is almost

certainly a lot less painful than staying unwell for the rest of your life.

✔ **Being passive.** Maybe if you wait long enough someone else will get better for you! Perhaps a miracle will happen to change your life, or a magic button will appear for you to push! Hey presto! – and you're fixed. Maybe, but don't hold your breath waiting. Take responsibility for doing the work needed to get you feeling better.

✔ **Having a fear of being bossed around.** Some people have a very strong sense of autonomy and they can be sensitive to other people trying to influence or coerce them. If you're one of these people, you may think that your therapist, or somebody close to you, is trying to take over when they suggest you try new strategies. Try to be open-minded to what professionals and people who care about you suggest. Deciding to give someone else's ideas a try is up to you. No one else can really control you or your decisions.

✔ **Being fatalistic.** Perhaps your motto is: 'This is the way I am and how I'm destined to be for all time.' Being convinced that your

(continued)

(continued)

moods are governed by forces beyond your control, such as chemicals, hormones, biology, the past, fate or God, means that you're prone to surrender yourself to your symptoms. Why not put your theories to the test by making a real effort to rewrite your supposed destiny? You never know: Your original assumptions may be wrong!

✔ **Love is the drug that I'm thinking of ...** You may be convinced that love is the only true path to happiness. You may be unable to imagine that you can have a satisfying life by learning to cope with your problems on your own. You may think that you will remain unhappy and emotionally disturbed until your special someone rides in on a steed to rescue you from this crazy mixed-up world. Love is a real bonus to human existence, make no mistake. However, the healthiest relationships are those where both parties are self-sufficient and enjoy the companionship of one another without being overly dependant.

✔ **Waiting to feel motivated.** A lot of people make the mistake of waiting to feel like doing something before they get started. The problem with waiting for inspiration, or motivation, is that you may hang about for far too long. Often, action precedes motivation. When overcoming emotional disturbance, you often need to do an experiment (check out Chapter 4) or you can stick to an activity schedule (in Chapter 9), even when doing so is the last thing that you feel like doing. Positive action is the best remedy for overcoming the feelings of lethargy and hopelessness.

Chapter 15

Psychological Gardening: Maintaining Your CBT Gains

*L*ooking after the positive changes you've made is a major part of helping you stay emotionally healthy. You can nurture your belief and behaviour changes every day. The process is a bit like watering a plant to keep it thriving. The more care you take of yourself both generally and specifically – for example, by practising your new ways of thinking and acting – the more you reduce the chances of returning to your old problematic ways.

This chapter provides tips and advice that can help you avoid relapses and manage setbacks if they do occur.

Knowing Weeds from Flowers

Think of your life as a garden. Unhealthy, rigid ways of thinking and corresponding behaviours like avoidance, rituals, safety strategies, perfectionism and trying too hard to please (to name but a few) are the weeds in your garden. The flowers consist of your healthy, flexible thinking, such as accepting yourself and others, accepting uncertainty and allowing yourself to be fallible, and your healthy behaviours, such as assertion, communication, problem-solving and exposure.

No garden's ever weed-free. Planting desirable plants isn't enough. You need to continuously water and feed the flowers, and uproot the weeds to keep your garden healthy. If you tend your garden regularly, the weeds don't get a chance to take hold because there you are with your trowel, digging 'em out at the first sign of sprouting. Depending on the virulence of your weeds, you may need to use some weedkiller from time to time in the form of appropriately prescribed medication. So, *know thy garden.*

To differentiate your weeds from your flowers, ask yourself the following questions:

- ✔ **What areas do I most need to keep working at in order to maintain my CBT gains?** The areas you identify are those where weeds are most likely to first take root.

- ✔ **What CBT strategies aid me most in overcoming my emotional problems?** Think about the new attitudes you've adopted towards yourself, the world and other people. These areas are your tender, new flowers – their delicate shoots need your attention.

- ✔ **What are the most useful techniques that I've applied to overcoming my emotional problems?** Think about the new ways of behaving that you've adopted (daffodils) and the old ways of behaving that you've dropped (thistles). Stick to your new, healthy behaviours and be vigilant against slipping back into your former unhealthy patterns of behaviour. Use an activity schedule to help you carry out beneficial routines and behaviours (jump to Chapter 9 for more about activity scheduling).

Write down the answers to the preceding questions so that you can look at them often to remind yourself of where to put in the hoe.

Working on Weeds

This section deals with weed-related topics and offers you some suggestions on how to stop them from taking over your garden, anticipating where they're likely to grow, and how to manage those that keep coming back.

Nipping weeds in the bud

Out of the corner of your eye, you see a weed sticking up its insidious little head. You may be tempted to ignore it. Maybe it'll go away or whither and die on its own. Unfortunately, weeds seldom eliminate themselves. Rather, they tend to spread and smother your burgeoning bluebells. Assume that any weed you identify needs savage and prompt killing.

A common reason for ignoring resurging problems is shame (which we talk about in Chapter 14). If you feel ashamed that your problems are recurring, you may try to deny it, and avoid seeking help from professionals or support from friends or family. You may be less likely to make a personal effort to whack down the problems in the way you did the first time.

Setbacks are a normal part of development. Human beings have emotional and psychological problems just as readily as physical problems. You don't have to be ashamed of your psychological problems, any more than you should be ashamed of an allergy or a heart condition.

Another common reason for people ignoring the reappearance of psychological problems is *catastrophising* or assuming the worst (head to Chapter 2 for more info on thinking errors). Many people jump to the conclusion that a setback equals a return to square one – but this certainly doesn't have to be the case. You can take the view that a problem you conquered once is at a fundamental disadvantage when it tries to take hold again. This is because you know your enemy. Use what you already know about recognising and arresting your old thinking and behaviour to help you pluck that weed before it gets too far above the ground.

Some emotional and psychological problems are more tenacious than others. Just because a problem's tenacious, it doesn't mean that it has to take over your life, or even cause you too much interference in it. However, you can expect to meet tenacious problems again. Keep up with treatment strategies even when your original problems are no longer in evidence; doing so will help prevent a relapse.

For example, if you have a history of depression, you may notice that weeds are popping up when you do some of the following:

- ✔ Begin to think in a pessimistic way about your future and your ability to cope with daily hassles.

- ✔ Ruminate on past failures and on how poor your mood is.

- ✔ Lose interest in seeing your family and friends.

- ✔ Have difficulty getting out of bed in the morning, and want to sleep more during the day instead of doing chores or taking exercise.

If you spot these stinging nettles making their way into your otherwise floral existence, try some of these techniques:

- ✔ Challenge your pessimistic thinking bias, and remind yourself that your thoughts are not accurate descriptions of reality but symptoms of your depression. (See Chapter 2 for more on thinking errors.)

- ✔ Interrupt the rumination process by using task-concentration techniques.

- ✔ Continue to meet with family and friends, despite your decreased interest, on the basis that doing so makes you feel better rather than worse.

- ✔ Force yourself out of bed in the morning and keep an activity schedule. (Have a read of Chapter 9 for more on activity schedules.)

Whatever your specific problems, follow the preceding example: write down your descriptions of anticipated weeds and some specific weed-killing solutions to have at hand.

Don't ignore signs that your problems are trying to get their roots down. Be vigilant. But also be confident in your ability to use the strategies that worked before and in your ability to use them time and again, whenever you need to.

Spotting where weeds can grow

To prevent relapse, become aware of where your weeds are most likely to take root.

Most people, regardless of their specific psychological problems, find themselves most vulnerable to setbacks when they're run down or under stress. If you're overtired and under a lot of environmental stress, such as dealing with work deadlines, financial worries, bereavement or family/relationship difficulties, you tend to be more prone to physical maladies, such as colds, flu and episodes of eczema. Psychological problems are no different from physical ones in this regard: they get you when you're depleted and at a low ebb.

You may notice that some problems are more evident when you're recovering from a physical illness. Recognising this common human experience can help you to combat any shame that you may feel, and to de-catastrophise a return of your symptoms.

Compile a list of situations and environmental factors that are likely to give your weeds scope to take on triffid-like power. For example, you may be able to pinpoint *environment triggers* for your depression, such as the following:

✓ Seasonal change, especially during autumn, when the days get shorter and the weather becomes colder.

✓ Sleep deprivation, due to work commitments, young children, illness or any other reason.

✓ Lack of exercise and physical activity.

✓ Day-to-day hassles piling up at once, such as the boiler breaking down in the same week that the washing machine explodes and a few extra bills arrive.

✓ Reduced opportunity for positive social interaction with friends and family.

You can also identify *interpersonal* triggers for your depression, such as the following:

✓ Tired and tetchy partner.

✓ Disagreements with your partner, children, parents or extended family.

✓ Critical or demanding boss.

✓ Disagreeable work colleagues.

Compile a list of high-risk situations for yourself, including situations that are most likely to fire up your unhealthy core beliefs (we explain core beliefs in Chapter 11), and situations that put you under strain. Creating such a list helps you to have a clear idea of when you're most vulnerable to relapse and identify which psychological soil is the most fertile for weed growth.

Dealing with recurrent weeds

Some weeds just seem to keep coming back. You may think you're rid of them, only to open your garden door to a scene from *Little Shop of Horrors* ('Feed me, Seymour!').

Some unhealthy beliefs are harder to erode than others. *Core beliefs* (refer to Chapter 11) are those that typically you've held to be true for a very long time – most of your life even. These beliefs will keep trying to take root and may be particularly resistant to your attempts to kill them off. The best way to deal with these recurrent weeds is to not become complacent. Keep reinforcing your alternative beliefs. Keep up with activities. Trust that over time and with persistence, your new ways of thinking and acting will get stronger.

Are you unwittingly feeding your weeds? Avoidance is a major weed fertiliser. You may have developed a healthy belief, such as 'I want to be liked by people, but I don't have to be. Not being liked by some people doesn't mean that I'm unlikeable.' And yet, if you still avoid social situations, self-expression and confrontation, you're giving your old belief that 'I must be liked by everyone or it means that I am an unlikeable person!', the opportunity to germinate.

Check out your reasons for avoiding certain situations and experiences. Are you not going to a party because you don't want to, or because you want to avoid the possibility of others judging you negatively in some way? Are you not visiting a farm because it doesn't interest you, or because you want to avoid contamination from pesticides?

When you spot a recurrent, mulish weed in your garden, dig it out from the root. You can kill off weeds entirely by getting the roots, *and* the shoots, out of the soil. Try not to make half-hearted efforts at challenging your faulty thinking. Dispute your thinking errors (Chapter 2) and push yourself back into challenging situations using your healthy coping strategies (we cover thinking errors in Chapter 2, and we talk about coping strategies in Chapters 4 and 11.)

Tending Your Flowers

Knowing when you're most prone to the symptoms of your original problems re-sprouting is one thing. But knowing how to troubleshoot problems and prevent weeds from growing back is another thing altogether.

The techniques, behavioural exercises and experiments that helped you to overcome your problems in the first place will probably work again. So, go back to basics. Keep challenging your negative thinking and thinking errors. Keep exposing yourself to your feared situations. If your life is in turmoil due to inevitable things like moving house, work difficulties or ill health, try to keep to your normal routine as much as possible.

Above all, even when things are going well, water your pansies! *Psychological watering* involves keeping up with your new ways of thinking and behaving, by giving yourself plenty of opportunity to consistently practise and test your new ways of living. As we mention in Chapter 11, healthy, alternative beliefs take time to become habitual. Be patient with yourself and keep doing healthy things, even when you're symptom-free.

Developing a plan for times of crisis is another good idea. Here are some examples of what you may wish to include in your plan to overcome a possible relapse:

✔ Consider seeing your GP or psychiatrist to determine whether you need to go on medication for a while.

✔ Talk about your feelings to someone you trust. Pick a person who you can rely on to be supportive. Seek the help of a professional if talking to a friend or family member isn't enough.

✔ Review your efforts from previous CBT work and re-use the exercises that were most effective.

✔ Keep your lifestyle healthy and active.

Planting new varieties

Digging out a weed (unhealthy belief and behaviour) is important, but you also need to plant a flower (healthy belief and behaviour) in its place. For example, if you notice that an old belief like 'I have to get my boss's approval, otherwise it proves that I'm unworthy' resurging, dispute the belief with arguments about the logic, helpfulness and truth of the belief. (Chapter 11 has more about disputing unhealthy beliefs.)

You also need to plant a healthy belief, such as 'I want my boss's approval, but I don't have to get approval in order to be a worthwhile person'. You can strengthen the new belief by gathering arguments for the logic, helpfulness and truth of the alternative healthy belief.

To strengthen new beliefs and behaviours further, you can devise situations that you know are likely to trigger your old unhealthy beliefs, and work at endorsing and acting according to your new beliefs instead. For example, deliberately seek your boss's feedback on a piece of work that you know is not your best. Resist your old behaviours that arise from the unhealthy belief that 'I must get my boss's approval', such as over-apologising or making excuses. Instead, accept yourself for producing a less than good piece of work and take note of constructive criticism (refer to Chapter 10 for more about self-acceptance, and head to Chapter 11 for more techniques to strengthen new beliefs).

You can dig out unhealthy behavioural weeds and plant behavioural flowers in their place. For example, you may note that you drink more alcohol in the evenings as your mood lowers with the shortening days. You know that the onset of winter gets you down because you spend more time in the house. You can make the choice to stop drinking more than one glass of wine in the evening and start going to a local dance class or some other activity instead. You can also make a list of activities to do indoors, which will keep you occupied during the winter evenings.

Plant flowers in place of weeds, and tend those flowers to keep them hardy. Your weeds will have greater difficulty growing again where healthy flowers are thriving.

A happy gardener's checklist

Here are some points to help you prevent and overcome relapse. Use this checklist to stop your marigolds getting choked by bindweed.

✔ **Stay calm.** Remember that setbacks are normal. Everyone has ups and downs.

✔ **Make use of setbacks.** Your setbacks can show you the things that make you feel worse as well as what you can do to improve your situation. Look for preventive measures that you may have used to get better, but that you may have let slide when your symptoms reduced.

✔ **Identify triggers.** A setback can give you extra information about your vulnerable areas. Use this information to plan how to deal with predictable setbacks in the future.

✔ **Use what you have learned from CBT.** Sometimes you think that a setback means that you're never going to get fully well, or that CBT hasn't worked for you. But if the stuff you did worked once, then chances are the same stuff can work again. Stick with it; you've nothing to lose by trying.

✔ **Put things into perspective.** Unfortunately, the more you've improved your emotional health, the worse black patches will seem in contrast. Review your improvement and try to see this contrast in a positive way – as evidence of how far you've come.

✔ **Be compassionate with yourself.** People often get down on themselves about setbacks. No one's to blame. You can help yourself get back on track by seeing a setback as a problem to overcome, rather than a stick with which to beat yourself.

✔ **Remember your gains.** Nothing can take your gains away from you. Even if your gains seem to have vanished, they can come back. You can take action to make this happen more quickly.

✔ **Face your fears.** Don't let yourself avoid whatever triggered your setback. You can devise further exposure exercises (refer to Chapters 12) to help you deal with the trigger more effectively next time it happens.

✔ **Set realistic goals.** Occasionally, you may experience a setback because you bite off more than you can chew. Keep your exercises challenging but not overwhelming. Break bigger goals into smaller, mini-goals.

✔ **Hang on!** Even if you aren't able to get over a setback immediately, don't give up hope. With time

(continued)

(continued)

and effort, you can overcome the setback. Don't hesitate to get appropriate support from friends and professionals if you think you need to. Remind yourself of times in the past when you felt as despairing and hopeless as you do now. Remind yourself of how you got out of the slump – and use the same strategies now.

Happy gardening!

Being a compassionate gardener

What do you do if one of your precious plants isn't doing so well? If you notice that you've got blight on your prize rose, do you deprive it of food and water, or do you try to treat the disease? It's better not to abuse or neglect the plants in your garden for failing to thrive because – if you do, they may only wilt further. You probably don't blame the plant for ill-health, so why should you blame yourself when you relapse?

Yes, take responsibility for anything that you may be doing that's self-defeating. And yes, accept responsibility for taking charge of your thinking, and ultimately, for engineering your own recovery. But, also take a compassionate view of yourself and your problems. Some of your unhealthy tendencies may have taken root partly due to childhood and early adulthood experiences. Others may have some biological underpinnings. Some of your problems may have arisen from a trauma. You're not alone in having emotional problems. You're part of the human race, and there is no reason to expect more of yourself than you do of others with regard to staying emotionally healthy.

How does your garden grow?

Research shows that CBT has a better relapse-prevention rate than medication on its own or other types of therapy. This difference may be because CBT encourages you to become your own therapist. Doing behavioural and written exercises does seem to help people to stay well, and for longer. Try to continue to be an active gardener throughout your life. Left to their own devises, most gardens become overrun with weeds. Think of maintaining the health of your psychological garden as an ongoing project.

If you take a responsible, compassionate view of setbacks, you will be more able to help yourself get well again.

You know that 'they' say you should talk to your plants to make them grow? Well, it may sound a bit daft, but maybe there's something in it. Try imagining yourself as a little pot plant on your kitchen windowsill. Talk to yourself encouragingly and lovingly when you notice your leaves drooping. Give yourself the types of messages that nurture rather than deplete you.

Part V
The Part of Tens

By Rich Tennant

I think it's really important for you to learn how to bounce back from these depressions.

In this part . . .

T his Part of Tens is a source of useful CBT information. You'll find ten fundamental pointers toward living in an upbeat and enjoyable way and ten ways to lighten up when things are getting you down.

Chapter 16

Ten Healthy Attitudes for Living

*T*his chapter offers ten rational philosophical standpoints that are good for your psychological health. Read them, re-read them, think them through and test out acting upon them to see for yourself.

Assuming Emotional Responsibility: You Feel the Way You Think

When you hold an attitude of personal responsibility for your feelings and actions, you're more able to find creative solutions, and your belief in your ability to cope with adversity is heightened. You empower yourself by focusing on your ability to influence the way you feel even if you can't control events.

On a cheerier note, when good things happen, you can also assess the extent to which they're a result of your own efforts – and then give yourself credit where due. You can appreciate good fortune without sabotaging your positive feelings with worries that your luck may run out.

Thinking Flexibly

Although circumstances may well be *desirable, preferable* and even *better* if the situation were different, they don't *have* to be a particular way. Accepting reality and striving to improve it where wise and achievable can help you save your energy for creative thought and action.

Valuing Your Individuality

You can express your individuality in many ways, such as in your dress sense, musical tastes, political opinions or choice of career. Yet perhaps you're hesitant to express your individuality openly because you fear the reaction of others. People who develop the ability to value their idiosyncrasies and to express them *respectfully* tend to be well-adjusted and content. Accepting that you're an individual and have the right to live your life, just as other people have the right to live theirs, is a pretty good recipe for happiness.

Accepting That Life Can Be Unfair

Life's unfair to pretty much *everyone* from time to time – in which case, perhaps things aren't as desperately unfair as you thought. If you can accept the cold, hard reality of injustice and uncertainty, you're far more likely to be able to bounce back when life slaps you in the face with a wet fish. You're also likely to be less anxious about making decisions and taking risks. You can still strive to play fair yourself, but if you accept that unfairness exists you may be less outraged and less horrified if and when justice simply doesn't prevail.

Understanding That Approval from Others Isn't Necessary

Accept yourself, independent of overt approval from other people in your life. Having a *preference* for being liked, appreciated and approved of by others – but not believing that you *need* approval – means that your self-opinion can be stable and you can weather disapproval. You may still behave in ways that are more likely to generate approval than disapproval, but you can also assert yourself without fear. You can consider praise and compliments a bonus rather than something you must cling to and work over-hard to maintain.

You cannot please all the people all the time – and if that's what you try to do, you're almost certainly going to be overly passive. If you can take the view that disapproval isn't the end of the world, intolerable and an indication that you're less than worthy, you can enjoy approval when you get it and still accept yourself when you don't.

Realising Love's Desirable, Not Essential

Some people would rather be in any relationship – even an unsatisfying or abusive one – than in no relationship at all. This need may stem from a belief that they can't cope with feelings of loneliness or get through life in general if they're alone. Other people consider themselves worthy or lovable only when they're reassured by being in a relationship.

Preferring instead of *demanding* to have a relationship helps you to retain your independence and individuality. Then when you *are* in a relationship, you're less likely to fall into the trap of trying to be the perfect partner – which means you can continue to attend to your own interests while being able to negotiate compromises when appropriate.

Tolerating Short-Term Discomfort

You *can* experience intense pleasure in the present and the future, but often some degree of pain and effort *today* are necessary to win you greater pleasure *tomorrow*. This will be true for many of the achievements you've already made in life. Putting up with temporary discomfort is also going to be crucial in *reducing* painful feelings of anxiety and depression. See Chapters 9, 12 and 13 for more on overcoming these problems.

Enacting Enlightened Self-Interest

Enlightened self-interest is about putting yourself first most of the time and one, two or a small handful of selected others a very close second. Enlightened self-interest is about looking after your own needs and interests while also being mindful of the needs of your loved ones and other people living on the planet.

Pursuing Interests and Acting Consistently with Your Values

Loads of evidence indicates that people are happier and healthier if they pursue interests and hobbies. Have you let your life become dominated by work or chores at home, and do you spend your evenings sitting in front of the television as a means of recharging? If your answer to this question is 'Yes!', then you're in extremely good, but not optimally healthy, company.

Tolerating Uncertainty

Healthy and productive people tend to be prepared to tolerate a degree of risk and uncertainty. Demanding certainty and guarantees in an uncertain world is a sure-fire recipe for worry and inactivity. Safety (or more accurately, the *illusion* of complete safety) comes at a cost – fewer rewards, less excitement, fewer new experiences.

Chapter 17

Ten Ways to Lighten Up

. . . .

In This Chapter

▶ Discovering the benefits of not taking things too seriously

▶ Finding yourself funny

▶ Getting more enjoyment out of life

▶ Throwing caution to the wind

. . . .

Sometimes you can make life more arduous than necessary by taking yourself too seriously. This chapter lists ten ways to lighten up a little, live with life's ups and downs and increase your overall enjoyment of things.

Accept That You Can – and Will – Make Mistakes

Consider the following attitudes to making mistakes:

> *Success is the ability to go from one failure to another with no loss of enthusiasm.*

(Sir Winston Churchill, British prime minister and statesman)

If you take yourself overly seriously, you're likely to consider your mistakes unacceptable. You may also believe that other people may reject you on the basis of your blunders. Moreover, you probably judge yourself harshly when you make a social gaffe or a poor decision. Remember that most of the time mistakes are a small price to pay for rich experiences.

Try Something New

Doing something foolish doesn't mean you're a fool. It's pretty much impossible for you to learn a new language or how to play the piano without making lots of grammatical gaffes or hitting the wrong notes. By giving yourself the opportunity to try new things, you may have a lot of fun in the process, even if you don't become a polyglot or a pianist in the Royal Philharmonic. Lots of things in life are worth doing simply for the sake of it!

Stamp on Shame

Taking yourself too seriously can lead you to experience unnecessary emotional upset. For example, if you need to look as though you're in complete control and composed all the time, you're a prime candidate for experiencing frequent bouts of shame.As one of your goals, you can have a go at overcoming your propensity to feel ashamed. Try deliberately exposing yourself to scrutiny using the following four-step technique:

1. **Make yourself conspicuous.** Wear a ridiculous outfit, make animal noises, or do anything else silly you can think of. Whatever you choose, do it *on purpose* and *in a very public place*.

2. **Stay in the situation long enough for your feelings of shame and general discomfort to subside on their own.** The important point is to stick with the exercise for whatever length of time it takes for you to feel *less* embarrassed, ashamed or anxious.

3. **Hold an attitude of self-acceptance throughout the experience.** Tell yourself that you can tolerate uncomfortable feelings, which you associate with possible negative evaluation from others.

4. **Repeat variations of the exercise often and without long gaps in between.** Try doing this exercise daily for a week; it's a great way to lessen your distress.

Laugh at Yourself

Many people claim that laughter's the best medicine. This adage may well carry a sizeable grain of truth. Finding the funny angle in an otherwise awkward situation can help remove the sting. Sometimes you can take the horror out of your mistakes and shortcomings by finding them amusing.

Don't Take Offence So Easily

If you believe that everyone must respect you and that you're only as good as what others think of you, then you're going to get offended if someone fails to appreciate you. You're pretty much destined to take offence much of the time unless you live in an air-conditioned bubble all on your own. Feeling offended is akin to feeling angry. Anger is tiring and unpleasant. Chances are that if you hold too serious a view of yourself, you're experiencing anger more often than you actually need to

Make Good Use of Criticism

Constructive criticism is a vital element of learning. Of course, not all the criticism you receive may be delivered in a skilled or constructive way. Nevertheless, if you can step back from negative feedback long enough to access its validity, you can use it to your advantage. Often, other people can see more clearly than you where you're going 'wrong' – others can have the benefit of an objective viewpoint.

Settle into Social Situations

To help yourself relax and be 'more yourself' in social settings, try these tips:

- ✔ **Focus your attention away from yourself and on to the other people present.** Really listen to the conversation and observe others.

- ✔ **Say things spontaneously.** Resist the urge to rehearse witty responses in your head before you speak. Take the risk of dropping in comments during the conversation.

- ✔ **Drop your safety behaviours** Avoid sitting on the outside of a group or fiddling with your drink, handbag or phone when conversation lulls. These types of behaviour stop you from getting used to natural social interaction.

✔ **Express yourself until you feel heard.** If you start to say something and are interrupted, try again in a few moments, maybe a little louder.

✔ **Rein yourself in.** If you tend to overcompensate for your social discomfort by talking a lot or putting on a bit of a show, give others the chance to fill in the gaps and silences.

✔ **Enjoy yourself.** Above all, remind yourself that social gatherings are meant to be fun. Make enjoying the company and conversation of other people your main reason for socialising.

You don't have to provide witty, imaginative or profound contributions to every topic of conversation. Don't decide that this means you're dull or uninformed generally!

Encourage Your Creativity to Flow

Creativity is self-generative: if you try out your ideas, they tend to give rise to more ideas. If you constantly suppress them, you may find that the stream of ideas diminishes over time.

Act Adventurously

Accepting your limitations to control events and to be certain about the outcome of events can help you to act more adventurously and live life more fully. Increasing your tolerance for uncertainty and limited control is also likely to help you become more adaptive when life throws unexpected problems your way.

Enjoy Yourself: It's Later than You Think

There's no time like the present for chilling out and lightening up. If you never get round to making time for pleasurable or novel activities, you may find that you don't ever do them. Making the most of the present moment can keep you young at heart, even as the years go by.

Index

FOR DUMMIES®

Making Everything Easier!™

UK editions

BUSINESS

Marketing Kit For Dummies
978-0-470-74490-1

Business Plans Kit For Dummies
978-0-470-74381-2

PRINCE2 For Dummies
978-0-470-71025-8

REFERENCE

British Politics For Dummies
978-0-470-68637-9

DIY For Dummies
978-0-470-97450-6

Researching Your Family History Online For Dummies
978-0-470-74535-9

HOBBIES

Growing Your Own Fruit & Veg For Dummies
978-0-470-69960-7

Allotment Gardening For Dummies
978-0-470-68641-6

Electronics For Dummies
978-0-470-68178-7

Anger Management
For Dummies
978-0-470-68216-6

Asperger's Syndrome
For Dummies
978-0-470-66087-4

Boosting Self-Esteem
For Dummies
978-0-470-74193-1

British Sign Language
For Dummies
978-0-470-69477-0

Cricket For Dummies
978-0-470-03454-5

Diabetes For Dummies,
3rd Edition
978-0-470-97711-8

Emotional Healing
For Dummies
978-0-470-74764-3

English Grammar
For Dummies
978-0-470-05752-0

Flirting For Dummies
978-0-470-74259-4

Football For Dummies
978-0-470-68837-3

Healthy Mind & Body All-in-One
For Dummies
978-0-470-74830-5

IBS For Dummies
978-0-470-51737-6

Improving Your Relationship
For Dummies
978-0-470-68472-6

Nutrition For Dummies,
2nd Edition
978-0-470-97276-2

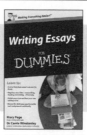

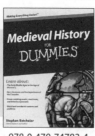

The easy way to get more done and have more fun

LANGUAGES

978-0-470-68815-1
UK Edition

978-1-118-00464-7

978-0-470-90101-4

MUSIC

978-0-470-48133-2

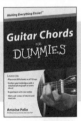

978-0-470-66603-6
Lay-flat, UK Edition

978-0-470-66372-1
UK Edition

SCIENCE & MATHS

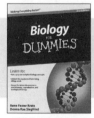

978-0-470-59875-7

978-0-470-55964-2

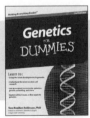

978-0-470-55174-5

Art For Dummies
978-0-7645-5104-8

Bass Guitar For Dummies, 2nd Edition
978-0-470-53961-3

Christianity For Dummies
978-0-7645-4482-8

Criminology For Dummies
978-0-470-39696-4

Currency Trading For Dummies
978-0-470-12763-6

Drawing For Dummies, 2nd Edition
978-0-470-61842-4

Forensics For Dummies
978-0-7645-5580-0

Index Investing For Dummies
978-0-470-29406-2

Knitting For Dummies, 2nd Edition
978-0-470-28747-7

Music Theory For Dummies
978-0-7645-7838-0

Piano For Dummies, 2nd Edition
978-0-470-49644-2

Physics For Dummies
978-0-7645-5433-9

Schizophrenia For Dummies
978-0-470-25927-6

Sex For Dummies, 3rd Edition
978-0-470-04523-7

Sherlock Holmes For Dummies
978-0-470-48444-9

Solar Power Your Home
For Dummies, 2nd Edition
978-0-470-59678-4

The Koran For Dummies
978-0-7645-5581-7

Wine All-in-One For Dummies
978-0-470-47626-0

Yoga For Dummies, 2nd Edition
978-0-470-50202-0

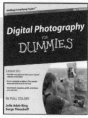
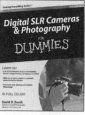